TEN FINGERS
TEN TOES
Twenty Things Everyone Needs to Know

NEUROPLASTICITY FOR CHILDREN

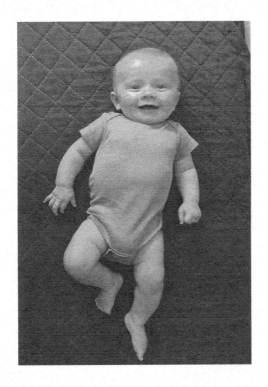

INSIDE SECRETS FROM A PHYSICAL THERAPIST
KAREN PRYOR
PhD, PT, DPT

Printed in the United States of America

ISBN: 978-1-54396-254-3 (print)

Published by BookBaby 7905 N. Crescent Blvd., Pennsauken, NJ 08110

Acknowledgements:

Illustrator/brain drawings by permission © Mica Foster DC

Baby pictures courtesy of Ashley and Luke Narramore

This book is for informational purposes only. It should not serve as a substitute for professional intervention from a qualified therapy professional; it should not be used to diagnose or treat any medical condition. Please consult with a physician or a neuroplasticity trained and qualified therapy professional before engaging in any activities in this book. The publisher and author of this book are not responsible or liable for any damages or consequences resulting from information found in it.

Some names and identifying details have been changed to protect patient privacy.

Dedication

This book would not have been possible without the support of my family. Sally, Mica, Jett, and Madison.

Thank you for believing in me.

Mom, Dad and Rick, my first teachers.

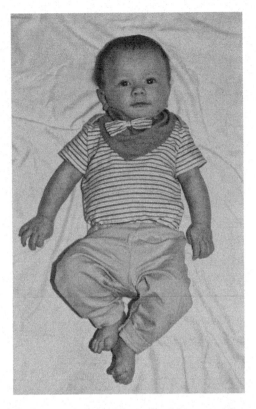

COMPASS – Navigating the Nervous System
through Neuroplasticity

Determine where the nervous system is working and not working

Decide where you want to go and progress.

A guide map for neural pathway development to increase function

For use at home with neuroplasticity trained
therapist instruction and treatment

Neuroplasticity certification available from
Karen Pryor PhD, PT, DPT

CONTENTS

Understanding
Neuroplasticity Principles
(neu-ro-plas-tic-i-ty)

Neuroplasticity is the ability of the nervous system to make new pathways and connections. This quality is especially useful in re-routing sensory information and processing around injuries or missing parts of the central nervous system. The brain constantly changes to form new routes or to prune unused connections.

Improved techniques and advances in neuroimaging have given us a greater understanding of how the central nervous system works. Let us embrace the progress of knowing what is working in the brain and what is not.

The nervous system pathways are altered by changes in type and location of sensory stimulation. Two of the influencers are sensation from the environment and emotional behavior. Most children who develop normally progress through major developmental milestones every two to three months for the first sixteen months of their lives. Each new activity builds on neural-musculoskeletal connections and communications. Many times the infant/child's body is perfect, but brain challenges have altered the demonstration of milestone attainment.

Therapists are able to customize nervous-system-targeted rewiring activities in conjunction with the precise testing results of MRI, FMRI, and CT scans, EEGs, and more. Cortex damage or impairments present with several options for treatment. One key option is to wire function to the side of the cortex that does not have impairments, by way of lower-level central nervous pathways (such as mammalian or reptilian brain functions). If a child is demonstrating a lower level of function than expected, more often than not the central nervous system is also functioning at that level. In motor milestone language, this means, for instance, that a child who cannot turn over may have functional connections in the reptilian brain level (brain stem), so therapy must start there. Or, a child who cannot balance or come to a sitting position may be functioning in the mammalian brain arena of connections. Applying the science of neuroplasticity is key to successfully identifying and attending to the specific level of brain development needed. It not only tells us how to medically treat the patient but also how to talk to them.

Because we can guide how the nervous system learns, we can also guide how the body develops. It is my intention in this book to share with medical practitioners neuroplasticity techniques that make positive changes in patients' development.

Foreword to Neuroplasticity

Some of the most challenging elements of treating patients are high or low tone and tremors. At some point in my medical career, I realized that if we could make tone more typical or normal and stop tremors in a patient—whether in a body part or in the eyes (nystagmus)—the patient would develop more typically.

Over the past forty years, I have found four hundred things or more that do *not* help patients heal. Because I've seen so much that does not work, my mission is to spread information about treatment that *does* work. I urge you to utilize the patterns, the sequences of brain development, and the totality of treating the child holistically, because only when the cause is addressed will the symptoms be reduced, easier to treat and the child will progress through motor milestones.

Most of the children we treat have typical /normal bodies, but their brains have been affected in ways that make their bodies act differently from the norm. This program named COMPASS, will assist in changing the brain in positive ways in order for the body to demonstrate greater voluntary control and higher milestone function. Ideally, treatment programs should be easy to understand by caregivers, practiced frequently, and updated after each therapy treatment.

C – Comprehensive Evaluation

O – Orientation
M – Mobility
P – Program and Purpose
A – Assessment of Results
S – Sensation
S – Symmetry

Everyone can make a difference in a child's life. I have spent most of my physical therapy career developing techniques to develop and rewire the brain. The vast majority of my patients have had neurological impairments as well as physical delays in development. High and low tone and visual challenges as well as tremors stood in the way of their motor function.

There is a force that assists in development of pathways for learning skills. You can be a guide of this force, helping to create neural pathway detours that connect viable cortical relay systems. This will produce changes in a patient's tone, place primitive reflexes in the background, and enhance higher motor skills.

Understanding the fundamentals of how children learn and grow is vital to helping them develop new skills. Each developmental milestone that a patient reaches is achieved through multiple elements of brain connections working together toward specific motor movements. Addressing those connections within the brain results in reduction of symptoms and more reliable progress of a child's developmental milestones and function. If a practitioner skips over multiple intricate connections, progress is delayed and substitution patterns are observed.

My experience with children who have special needs began early in life. When I was sixteen years old, I taught swimming classes at the Little Rock YWCA. One of my classes was filled with children with special needs. Being a competitive swimmer, not only did I have to reach back in time to my knowledge of underwater basics—such as blowing bubbles through my nose and floating—I also had to figure out basic body movements and elements of motion desired in children who had various challenges. Fortunately, the children were patient with me, as I was with them. I learned how to teach them at their specific learning levels, and they learned how to swim.

The techniques I used to discern what level each toddler or child could move and learn are still valuable today. Understanding the neurological development of infants gives us a new perspective on a person's lifelong physical and mental development. Think of the infant's brain as a roadway being built. Neurological pathways begin as rough trails. Increased traffic on these trails creates more defined paths. These paths develop into roads, and the roads develop into high-speed highways. The development of these neurological pathways depends completely upon the reinforcement and frequency of usage of these neural connections.

Daily practice of something new is required to increase the traffic on these neurological pathways, leading to the development of skills. The earlier a patient begins developing these neurological pathways, the faster development will occur. It is important that the caregiver observes, practices, and works on activities with the child in their home all week. Practice makes pathways. While neurological development is most active early in life, these concepts can be applied to older children and adults as well.

To paraphrase the philosopher Heraclitus, no man steps into the same river twice, for it's not the same river and he's not the same man. Likewise, one cannot step into the same nervous system twice because experience causes constant change. The conscious therapist is constantly learning. It is my mission to educate all individuals who have direct contact with babies and children, especially children with developmental delays, about the hope of neuroplasticity to effect positive change. By being aware of the challenges children face, we have a greater opportunity to reduce developmental delays and to help develop the mind and functional abilities. Together we can make a positive difference that will last a lifetime.

Enjoy watching positive changes!

—Karen Pryor, PhD, PT, DPT

Introduction to Neuroplasticity

Studies show that experience can rewire our brains and enhance new learning possibilities. In some cases, it acts as an adaptive mechanism to compensate for lost function or to maximize function in the event of brain injury. As therapists, when we treat the causes and symptoms of these motor delays, we can utilize alternate brain pathways to improve the effects of therapy. Neuroplasticity changes brain connections and, hence, changes motor and cognitive functions.

Learn how therapy can change the brain and how neuroplasticity can change the challenges in a child's development. From congenital abnormalities to traumatic brain injuries, this book delivers new and exciting ideas for detouring around damage and incorporating viable nervous system connections with tools you can use. I will act as your guide to assist you in gaining a deeper understanding of multisensory experiences that forge and shape connections in the central nervous system. New connections wire to functional pathways and progress is evident in improved motor skills.

The therapy techniques learned in this book, addressing both high and low tones, can be easily integrated into the clinic or home. They are also teachable to parents and caregivers as a different way of playing. Children will play longer than they will work. Be sure you videotape case studies in slow and regular speed to analyze your patients' changes. As we all know, one cannot go back in time. The videos will serve as a record of changes before and after integrative neuroplasticity treatments.

In the past, therapists hoped their patients' adverse health conditions would change by using various therapy techniques such as splinting, bracing in standing. We are now using neuroplasticity to inform the way we modify brain connections to change how the body works. In this book, we will be concerned with genetics, injuries, and missing portions of the central nervous system of the fetus/infant/child. Techniques to address these issues work for all ages. In the very young, they tend to work fast, sometimes in as little as sixty minutes.

There are multiple motor challenges involved in treating the child/infant. Many of the atypical symptoms are spasticity/hypertonia, hyponia, torticollis athetoid, tremors, gross motor dysfunction, obligatory primitive reflexes, and the list goes on. These abnormal symptoms may be demonstrated in misalignment of head and neck, difficulty with rotation of trunk, and poor coordination of bilateral upper and lower extremities. This is where we come face to face with the child's lack of attaining developmental milestones.

I will guide you through how the brain connects, how it adds new connections with exercises to make progressive therapy fun, faster and more rewarding. We will take a journey through the nervous system and neuroanatomy. Then jump into how the brain can change tone, movement, and key sensory functions that are initiators of change in the brain.

This information will assist you in how therapy can change the brain and how neuroplasticity can reduce the challenges in child development. You will gain creative evidence-based approaches to incorporate into a multisensory experience to drive home the importance of diverse and novel activities during treatment sessions. This information can be easily integrated into clinic, school, and home treatment program.

Neuroplasticity
for Children

Studies show that our brains can be rewired to enhance new learning. Functional MRI scans demonstrate firing pathways and damaged areas. The picture seems a far cry from traditional hands-on treatment. How can therapists reach into the nervous system and change its pathways? With so many possible types of nervous system issues, our challenge is how to determine which specific treatments will match the presenting issues. No one lives in a textbook, and commonly accepted protocols do not always fit a child's needs. No child is neurologically identical to another child, even in the case of identical twins. Consider the case of how experiences change the nervous system moment by moment and movement by movement. As therapists we have to think on our feet and re-evaluate the child each day for the treatment needed each session.

In some cases, abnormal patterns of motor skills are demonstrated by a child as a reflection of the part of the central nervous system that possesses the abruption of pathways. Compensation is the drive of the child to work around the impairments and accomplish motor tasks. Intense COMPASS work directed below the level of damage results in neurological rewiring of function. These abnormal motor patterns are a demonstration of substitution relay systems within the central nervous system. They are exhibited as decreased or increased tone, tremors and primitive reflexes. Hopefully, this book will allow you to evaluate the child and move forward on appropriate available pathways that can detour around damage and connect.

As therapists, we primarily have power in the sensory realm of experience for the child. Feedback loops assist in rewiring the motor responses. When we work on the cause and central nervous system location of dysfunction through targeted neurological sensory treatments, the symptoms of these motor delays diminish. Utilization of alternate brain pathways serves to improve the effectiveness of therapy. Therapists will be aware of pathways available for cross connections. Neuroplasticity is primary in changing brain connections and hence, changing motor and cognitive functions. From congenital abnormalities to traumatic brain injuries, this book delivers new and exciting ideas on how to detour around damage, how to intentionally guide and incorporate viable nervous system connections.

Learning how therapy can change the brain and how neuroplasticity can change the challenges in a child's development will revolutionize progress with patients. As you examine scans of the child, look with new eyes. Place neurological level of developmental milestones alongside the impairments. This will help you build programs for the children you treat. Each child changes daily and updating a multisensory-motor experience drives home the importance of diverse and novel activities. Video case studies are available in the seminars given by Karen Pryor PhD, PT, DPT and demonstrate changes before and after integrative neuroplasticity treatments and the COMPASS program. The therapy techniques learned in this book can be easily integrated into the child's program.

We are now using the word neuroplasticity; the way we can modify brain connections to change how the body works. In the past, we worked on the body with various therapy techniques, splinting, bracing, standing and hoping conditions would change. The child looked like they were in an improved position, but we covered their sensory endings so much that it inhibited the brain-body learning experience. We now realize the brain can rewire so dependence on support structures may be reduced. For years there has been extensive research and visible proof that neuroplasticity occurs. Now is the time for advanced skills to utilize this information and promote rewiring of the nervous system for improved outcomes. There are multiple motor challenges faced when treating the young child/infant.

Many of the atypical symptoms such as hypertonia or hyponia, relate to cortical or midbrain impairment. When the cortex has damage, the lower centers are more active. Primitive reflex patterns interfere with voluntary movements, primarily live in the lower brain areas and must be addressed there. Other abnormal symptoms of torticollis or high tone may be demonstrated in misalignment of head and neck. This presents with difficulty relating to rotational movements of the eyes, trunk and rolling over. This is only one area where we come face to face with lack of achievement of the developmental milestones.

With a journey through neuroanatomy you will be able to see how nervous system processing is layered and how to address treatments. Understanding how the brain connects, processes and interprets stimulation is essential for how it adds new connections. Complete connections are required for appropriate motor responses and initiation of movement. Knowledge of neurosensory movement theory in COMPASS assists the therapist in exercise program development and to make progressive therapy fun, faster and more rewarding. The therapist can then update the program to fit the level of the child that day. Then move into how the brain can change tone through prolonged or reduced sensation. Attention to key sensory functions and movement are initiators of change in the brain.

This book will help you drive the neuroplasticity brain train effect with your patients, through switching stations, nuclei, short and long neural pathways. The validation is noted in the results of therapy sessions and parent daily practice. Neurological evaluation and techniques addressed will assist the therapist in deciding which techniques to use. Neuroplasticity may change brain connections as well as change motor and cognitive functions.

External bracing that covers parts of the body in need of stimulation can act as a shield to the integration process by reducing the amount of sensation that enters the nervous system. The nervous system, ligaments, muscles may not accelerate functionally if continuously covered by an ankle foot orthosis. High or low tone is a brain challenge. Change in the brain connections will allow increased function with minimal, on-off or no bracing. In our clinic we provide alignment of the foot in the shoe with dynamic gel support or on-off bracing with positive results.

All individuals learn from sensory experiences. Even when there are active motor movements, the information coming into the central nervous system is sensory. Neuroplasticity guidance allows for correction, alteration, and success in gross and fine motor behaviors. Novel activities relay new pathways and connections. Repetition, instruction, and practice strengthen the connections, which in turn move the cortical engagement to become more of an automatic response and subconscious action. With decreased use of pathways, they weaken and may eventually be pruned. Neuroplasticity is an inside job.

Beginning with initial evaluation then moving from reflex to voluntary function, the information in this book delivers new methods on how to rewire around damage and utilize viable nervous system connections. There are various levels of stimulation. The body's motor demonstration reacts differently depending on the nervous system's ability to interpret sensation. Sensation takes a journey and is monitored through the reticular formation, parietal lobe and processed through multiple nuclei throughout the central nervous system. Motor reactions and responses vary in relation to gravity alterations; position in space; and acceleration, deceleration and direction of head, neck, trunk, and/or extremities. The amount, length of time, and type of stimulation also change primitive reflex pattern strength as well as high and low tone presentation in patients.

We must always remember that the brain is plastic and able to change structure and function. Neurogenesis is the production of neurons. Beginning the third week of gestation, 250,000 neurons per minute are formed until birth. Neuron production continues throughout the lifespan although at a slower rate. Neurogenesis was discovered at the Salk Institute in San Diego in a seventy-two-year-old individual.

Consideration of a patient's history, pre-natal experience, environmental conditions, neonatal abstinence syndrome, birth injury, genetic disorders, ACE score and other information assists the therapist in including specific treatments to rewire connections. Realizing what is working and what is not functioning appropriately serves as the basis for a therapy program that will suit the specific needs of the child and increase the potential for neuroplasticity to occur optimally.

Sensory education within the body and central nervous system is when stimulation is received and lays down information. Sensory re-education is a rerouting of novel neural information to assist a person in responding appropriately to sensory experiences. Thus, information can be rerouted through different types of sensation. Therapists often guide motor movements, but once we visualize the active pathways in our mind, we see sensation goes in to be interpreted and motor function is sent out for action. Correction occurs through feedback loops to improve motor movements. So if you are treating a patient and feel their movement is not effective for the skill desired, change your hand placement and sensations delivered. For example, hold a patient's wrist and elbow (carpals and condyles) for proprioceptive reception rather than forearm and hand, which triggers primitive reflex patterns and muscle contractions.

Peter Breggin's book *Talking Back to Ritalin* (2001, pp. 62-81) reveals that central stimulants can cause brain cell damage in growing children. He is a proponent of education rather than medication. In the book Harald Blomberg, MD author of *Movements That Heal,* (2015) reported that rhythmic movement can be much more effective in helping children with ADHD than some medications.

Sometimes medications are necessary, and this book can work with medication use. We need to analyze, however, what each medication does and how it affects patients' motor and sensory systems. Some anti-spasticity medications, for instance, decrease sensation. Sensation reception and processing is how we all learn. Natural sensory stimulation and entry into the nervous system can change neural connections in ways that lead to more typical behavior without the side effects of multiple medications. If we can decrease tone in children with spasticity without using medications, we may accomplish more functional motor skills.

And so, through case studies we begin a journey together into the nervous system to describe ailments, deficiencies, misconnections, deletions of parts of the brain, genetic anomalies, trauma, and other insults that shape the way the brain and body function.

Children with cerebral palsy may demonstrate obligatory primitive reflexes and pathological or absent postural reactions. *Pediatric Neurology* conveyed the importance of combined evaluation of primitive and postural reflex assessments to predict early identification of delayed development. (Dimitrios and Zafeiriou Volume 31, Issue 1, pp1-8) Substance of evidence can be documented by photo and video as the child progresses. As therapists, we know - what is obvious to you is obvious to you and can also be video evidence of challenges and progress.

This makes perfect sense. Primitive reflexes live in a lower brain center than postural responses and voluntary movements. If there is damage in the cortex, lower centers take over and demonstrate changes in tone, making the appearance of primitive reflexes obligatory. Neuroplasticity-based treatments form neural connections to higher-level functioning pathways in the midbrain and cortical regions. As a result, the primitive reflexes are no longer needed for basic movements. Connections to the cortical functions then override use of lower centers that previously impaired function and voluntary movement. The central nervous system actually prefers to use higher-level centers because doing so uses less energy in the brain and body as well as being more effective and efficient.

The sooner therapists can screen children, begin integrative therapy treatments, and promote developmental progression through neuroplasticity techniques, the more connections the children form to higher-cortex pathways and the better the results. If you need additional information on how the brain can network information for improved results, consider taking my seminars in Neuroplasticity.

Many therapy techniques discuss inhibition of primitive reflexes which form during fetal life. In a 12-14 week old embryo the nerve cells are forming around 15 million per hour.

https://www.ncbi.nlm.nih.gov/books/NBK234146/ - ddd00048
retrieved 010318

If there is any developmental interference by medication, genetics, nutrition, toxic materials, or birth trauma, retention of primitive reflexes may be noted. Neuroplasticity can rewire the nervous system in such a way that new pathways are formed around damage areas and connect to viable neurological synapses. Therefore, integration of the primitive reflex responses is via sensory stimulating activities and exercises. This will demonstrate more active functional motions and the release of obligatory pathological physical movements with abnormal tonal qualities. The brain is able to modulate, filter, and interpret all the varieties of sensation. This information is routed via receptors from sensory pathways and directed to the incoming connections in the brainstem, midbrain and cortex. Sensation is the pathway into the central nervous system. Motor pathways exit the central nervous system and are demonstrated in voluntary and involuntary motor movements.

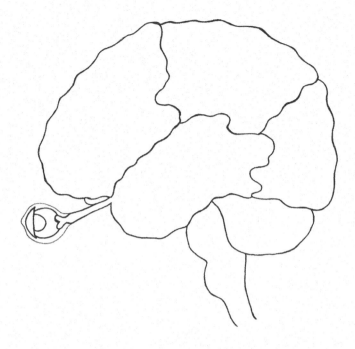

All drawings used with permission from © Mica Foster DC

Infant Brain

The infant brain forms pathways through sensory experiences. In utero, a five-month fetus hears their mother speaking. Through movements, the fetus receives sensory information. Reflexive movements of neck, trunk, arms, and legs begin to connect sensation and motor pathways. There is an urgent need to start as early as possible after birth to progress therapeutic interventions with Neuroplasticity techniques.

Baby's Brain Begins Now: Conception to Age 3

The brain is not a completely blank slate at birth: Light has entered the eyes. Sounds of the Mother's native language have passed through the placenta and into the fetal ears. Movements of the fetus have assisted in developing neural connections of pressure on body parts. Infants are affected by their surroundings before and after birth. Birth can be a traumatic experience in itself. Whether C-section or vaginal birth, the infant is delivered from a fluid filled floating experience to enter a land defined by gravity forces.

Child development specialists have written decades of findings about how environment affects children long-term. Experience connects information and relay systems in the central nervous system. Neglect, low caregiver interaction and stimulation of the child have negative effects on school performance. (Neurons to Neighborhoods: The Science of Early Childhood Development pp182-217)

This book shows how an infant's senses can be stimulated and rewired for optimum function. Recognition and reduction of adverse childhood experiences go a long way in improving neurological function and health. Neuroplasticity techniques assist the practitioner in reaching into the nervous system to connect synaptic function for optimum fine and gross motor skill performance.

Recent progress in imaging and testing has provided an idea of how stress, environment, nurture, and neglect may influence early brain development. With these images, neuroscientists are able to identify various patterns in brain activity. These appear to be associated with different types of experiences. (Akerman,S. Raichle,M. Discovering the Brain, 34-45)

Long-term effects of early stress, poverty, neglect, and maltreatment were well documented years before we could "see" them with brain scanning tools. We need an understanding of intricate brain development, stages, levels, and reflexes to help us rewire damage and the effects of neglect to the nervous system.

What can we do about these negative long-term effects? Identify the cause/s and provide treatment. Symptoms will be reduced when the cause is remedied. Stress lives in the subconscious mind, and all activities need to be in line with subcortical functions. Sensory stimulation through cranial nerve transmission reaches into subcortical structures. Remove the fight or flight stimulation such as chaotic rooms that are full of loud noise and/or too much light. Therapists must rewire patients' reactions of fight, flight, freeze, or faint so their adverse responses are reduced. These responses reside in lower brain centers and may have effects in an overpowering way. If the lower centers are stimulated, responses can interfere with higher centers of active motion and learning: one cannot run from a lion and read a book.

There are several reasons why we should learn from the evidence of neuroscience. Neuroscientists assist us in knowing how and when experiences affect children. There are specific times of vulnerability to certain types of experiences, and when we as therapists understand these patterns, we can improve our therapy intervention. There are windows of opportunity for optimum rewiring, and if a child misses the "neurological optimum window"—for instance, learning to walk between ten months and sixteen months—it is much harder to attain the expected skill outside of that timeframe.

It is imperative to teach caregivers an easy-to-understand, sensory, and motor program for home use. Written, practiced, and demonstrated with the baby in hand is essential. Toys and equipment in the home can be used daily for developmental progression and increased motor control. If your facility has a "no parents beyond this point" policy, it is impairing the progress of the child. Parents may not understand a summary of the treatment session. Usually therapies are not in a caregiver skill set. Please bring the parent/s in and let them practice treatments for their children with you.

The parent working on the therapy program at home daily will promote the child's progress. In spite of all of the brain studies in existence, it is still a mystery how exactly the mind learns and develops routes of habituation on the cellular level. We do know generally, that trails of conduction and synapses are used or pruned. We also know that therapeutic methods can send in sensation and drive motor information that result in changes in development.

Therapists face increasing changes in reimbursement, workload in school systems, and challenges in obtaining referrals for the very young patient. In light of these challenges, we must devise methods that change the brain quickly for appropriate motor-movements evaluation scores to align with typical children. Evaluations must look beyond motor milestones and consider neurologic impairments as a process indicator to get the therapy started now.

Jean Ayres developed the *Sensory Integration and the Child* book to aid children in reaching new heights in motor function. These techniques treat visual, motor, body awareness through touch and coordination training. Sensory integration is a function of the nervous system receiving sensations and then processing the resulting information. Sensory processing describes how sensation is received, transmitted, and interpreted. The integration of information, due to deficits in these pathways may be impaired and are rendered as abnormal movement patterns.

Neuroplasticity utilizes the information of typical perception of sensory information and achievement of functional responses and movement. The progression of intense use of specific sensory attention with positioning stimulation increases the realm of neuroplasticity. It aids in re-organization of the atypical central nervous system function to deliver more typical movement patterns and milestone attainment.

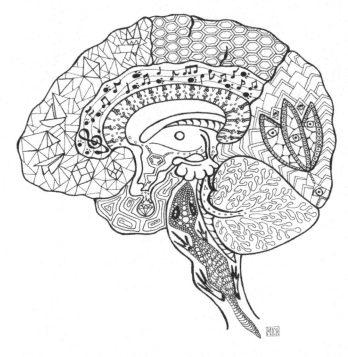

© Mica Foster DC

We begin with an outline of brain anatomy. This will be followed by a deeper understanding of the brain's layers and how one can promote new functional connections. The earlier the treatment begins, the better. In diagraming the brain, note the brainstem, midbrain, and cortex and how these three layers are built upon one another. If the cortex is injured, the midbrain, pons, medulla or commonly called brain stem become prominent in displays of primitive motor functions and abnormal tone.

The brain stem houses most of the cranial nerve attachments, III-XII as well as primitive reflexes. This area low in the central nervous system also monitors and regulates homeostasis. Temperature, heart rate, breathing, intake of nutrients, and hydration are essential to life. If the infant is hungry, stroking the cheek stimulation results in the infant's head, neck turn and rooting reflex. This is typically followed by sucking and swallowing. Reflexes for survival are housed in the brain stem.

The brain stem is sometimes called the reptilian brain. Most reptiles have difficulty rolling over or balancing in sitting. Think of the alligator. Rotation of the limbs and trunk is limited in this deep level of the nervous system. Rotation ability is required for control of balance. Some elements of rotation components in rolling, coming to a sitting position, balance and rudiments of ambulation are processed in the mammalian area.

If you see a child that possesses the inability to rotate or balance, they may be operating in the brain stem. The eyes of a reptile can also work independently of each other. Likewise, some of the children we treat have difficulty with eye teaming.

The mammal brain is superior to the brainstem, with more complex functions. Sometimes known as the limbic system, it includes the hippocampus, amygdala, cingulate cortex, and hypothalamus. Emotion forges pathways through the limbic system and touches both hemispheres of the brain from the inside. Spatial navigation, emotional regulation and memory are some of the functions of the hippocampus. Length and depth of sleep can affect the memory function of the hippocampus. Amygdala assists the nervous system in detecting fearful situations. The cingulate gyrus surrounds the corpus callosum and lies underneath the cortex. It is involved with emotion and behavior processes and regulation. The hypothalamus controls activities in the Autonomic Nervous System and pituitary gland.

Here in the mammal brain, let's think of a dog's functional abilities. Dogs understand short bits of sentences that pertain to the present: come, sit, stay, play, and all done. In the same way, the mammal/subconscious mind also is in the "here and now." This is one reason the word "no" may have little effect on actions arising from the limbic system. The limbic system does not wear a watch. In other words, it is a brain based time free zone. This is the primary reason a toddler is unable to conceive the information about going to swim at 1:00 pm or in 2 hours. Small children also have difficulty comprehending the concept of "No". "No" refers to something done in the *past* that we don't want done again. It can also mean, don't do that in the *future*. Redirection works well with children functioning from the mammal brain because it is a "right now" activity.

The cortex has multiple lobes and left and right hemispheres. For our purposes in this book, we will give each lobe qualities that target pathway formation into new territories:

- Frontal lobe – emotion

- Temporal lobe – hearing, vestibular, speech/language, procedural tasks

- Parietal lobe – sensory, motor, feedback loops of sensory and motor, processing

- Occipital lobe – sight, vision, coordination of visual tracking, focus, and processing

- Cerebellum (lobe) – included here because of importance, smooth motion in motor movements, coordinates with motor function.

To Change One Life

Jason's Story

It was one of those hot summer days in rural Tennessee where the humidity hung so heavy in the air that the silver maple trees curled their leaves in anticipation of the showers that were forecast for the afternoon. Walking through the parking lot outside of my office, I agreed with the trees that it was time for the rain to come. The breeze that blew across my face carried with it the scent of a summer storm.

Entering the waiting room, I realized that someone was already there. I smiled a general greeting in their direction, intending to continue into my office to start my day, when something stopped me in my tracks. It was the look in the mother's eyes. That look of desperation was heart-wrenching. In her lap sat a small baby, sporting short, brown hair and his mother's brown eyes, but unlike a typical infant, his neck was limp in her arms, with tiny fists pulled to his chest and legs that were outstretched and rigid. Next to mother and child sat an older woman, the child's grandmother. I laid my paperwork behind my desk and walked briskly toward the trio with my hand outstretched, introducing myself. I responded to their introductions, but that was as far as the small talk would progress.

Placing a hand on my arm, the mother said, "We've been everywhere, and everyone tells us something different. One neuro-ophthalmologist said my son was born blind and he cannot use his arms and legs. He has cerebral palsy."

I invited them to come back to the exam room. They followed with their stroller, diaper bags, and blankets. I could tell that the mother was having a hard time holding her baby because of the child's inability to move his body into a cuddle position to conform to the shape of her arms. As we reached the exam room, the mother handed me her child and turned to leave with the child's grandmother. "I would like you to stay during the examination and therapy session," I stated as they paused at the door.

With wide eyes, the grandmother offered, "The other physical therapist we went to didn't like for us to stay."

"Yeah," agreed the mother. "They had a sign above the door that said, 'No parents beyond this point.' You mean you don't work that way?"

"I certainly DO NOT work that way," I said trying very hard to hold in my frustration with the detachment procedures that some practitioners still cling to. "I want you to be present during the treatments so you can work with your baby at home. It makes no sense at all to practice only one to two hours a week with your therapist on special exercises that can reformat and rewire the brain. I want you to work on his program every day as much as possible because the brain remembers whatever is done the longest."

The adults both physically relaxed, and I handed baby Jason back to his mother. I further explained that the treatments would follow in a step-by-step progression. For example, a child's ability to sit up relies on completion of many smaller steps first. They, as the parents, would work with their child on each new skill until he accomplished it.

"And it won't feel like work," I assured them. "In fact, most parents and babies enjoy it. They think they are playing." I walked over to the child's small, spastic body and examined him as his mother held him close. His small, brown eyes moved in different directions, but it was evident that he could hear everything we were saying. When I grabbed a noisy toy, he turned his head toward it. I then had his grandmother hold him, and I asked his mother to walk in a different direction. The child followed the sound of her voice. Clearly, he was using the senses that he had to bring information into the sensory system about the world. I performed co-joined exercises to wire vision and hearing together. Then they practiced the skills.

To look at Jason in his current state was to see a child who was almost frozen in a moment of fight-or-flight. When I tried to extend his arms and uncurl his fingers, it was difficult and his palms were moist. With a basic understanding of his condition, we got to work.

Partnering with his grandmother, mother, grandfather, and father, Jason was exposed to activities, motions, sights, sounds, positions, and lighting daily. We cheered when he demonstrated decreased tone in his arms and fingers and was able to reach out and grasp a favorite toy. With the freedom of active movement and additional sensation experiences introduced to an open hand, he began an avid exploration of the sensations of soft, rough, cold, vibrating and noisy toys. Reaching into the world where sound and touch were his teachers, he became more and more curious about his surroundings.

And then he laughed. I watched as his mother's eyes welled up with tears as she heard the happy sound of her son. It was as if the uncurling of his fingers had been a signal to the rest of his spirit. I knew that this was indeed the case when he was able to control his eyes and to watch his mother as she walked across the room during a treatment session. Next in succession, he sat up, looked around, and could pick up and throw a toy. Finally, he was able to reach out and feed himself.

When Jason returned to his follow-up appointment with the pediatric neuro-ophthalmologist, the Doctor leaned across the desk after his assessment and told the parents that he did not know what had happened. The child could see and did not need glasses, and his future appointments would be cancelled. This child who was labeled as disabled and blind had parents who refused to give up and who kept searching for additional therapies. Their fighting spirit became his fighting spirit, and, I don't mind telling you, made me his biggest fan.

The reason I include Jason's story (and later on the stories of other children), is to show you that each patient is not a protocol, a procedure, or a product that can be easily fit into a one-size- fits-all treatment. No one lives in a textbook. As each child is different and may face multiple challenges, each treatment must rise to that level of uniqueness. If we don't understand this as therapists and caregivers, we miss the incredible honor of witnessing and being a part of some of the most courageous and phenomenal moments a person can experience. To help another human being access their ability to connect with the world is a privilege that we all strive to be worthy of.

An Act of Connecting

Research indicates that the way medical personnel deliver a diagnosis can affect the parents' attitudes both toward their child and toward healthcare professionals. Taking a few minutes to adequately and compassionately explain a child's diagnosis and the why and how of a treatment program can go a long way toward the parents understanding and moving toward assisting their child with his or her therapy. This will also help with compliance in the exercise program.

Compliance and daily practice are necessary for advancing the child's brain rewiring and synaptic connections to increase developmental skills. If caregiver activities are performed daily, progress will happen. If there is little to no caregiver involvement with therapy, progress does not happen, or it happens extremely slowly. It's that simple. I often ask parents if they want to work hard for two years or for the rest of their lives. You can imagine their answer.

Onboard caregivers revolutionize the child's developmental acceleration. Simple movements, sensory stimulation, and a basic understanding of the nervous system is important for knowing the *why* of what to do. We teach parents, grandparents, aunts, uncles, cousins, brothers, sisters, nurses, childcare providers, teachers…the list goes on. We are all in this together.

When I meet with new patients and their families for the first time, I tell them that my purpose is not only to help the patients learn how to move better but also to teach them how to continue their therapy at home in order to accelerate their progress. In short, successful therapy begins with the therapist at the clinic, school or home and continues with the caregiver at home. Daily practice of active home programs literally changes the way the brain develops by engaging developing neurological pathways. Daily family engagement is vital to accelerated developmental progress.

Many families are overwhelmed with higher-than-expected level of care needed for their child at home. In the hospital, two to three shifts of professionals are available to work with the baby. Home care is one shift, twenty-four hours a day, seven days a week. Be proactive about avoiding caregiver fatigue by offering simple and effective treatments for the child in the home setting. We all want progress, and being proactive in this way will give the best potential outcome for the whole family. Usually caregivers want to be confident and competent in helping their child.

Try to integrate the exercises into a patient's daily routine care. For example, teach manual therapy and sensory stimulation techniques while the patient is dressing or bathing. It is vital that the caregivers watch every therapy session, practice the activities with the therapist, and receive feedback. In what I call the *PT Phone Home* program, videos of the exercises of the caregiver and the child can be used on an ongoing basis in the patient's home exercise program practice. Consider, for instance, a person cannot learn to play piano with lessons one time a week. They need a piano and sheet music to practice at home. Daily practice is key.

To help keep patients and caretakers engaged in therapy, the exercises in this book incorporate the concepts of neuroplasticity into playtime with a program I call "Educated Play." This program explains how every activity in which the patient is engaged serves to increase nervous system connections and physical development. In my clinic, I have found that seemingly miraculous developments occurred when parents and caregivers were given easy-to-follow instructions and opportunities to work with their babies with everyday special activities.

Babies and young children are constantly exploring the world around them. They rely primarily on their senses of touch and sight to gain a sense of their surroundings and develop neurological pathways. They are dependent on adults to provide them with not only food and care but also learning opportunities. Since these at-home Educated Play sessions are enjoyable and stress-free, they encourage the patient's nervous system to learn and grow more quickly.

Babies who spend time on their tummy while awake are assisting their nervous system in multiple neurological ways. This basic posture results in visual, auditory, and vestibular pathway stimulation that sends information into the brain to be processed and judged successful and useful or not. Shifting body weight in relation to gravity is an imperative precursor for children to develop control of their head, neck, trunk, arm, and leg placement. Proprioceptor detectors in joints send information into the balance coordinates. Coordination between balancing, rotary components, and weight bearing on trunk, arms, and then legs forms the neuro-motor basis for progressing through several developmental milestones.

Making therapy activities fun is vital because children and adults will play longer than they will work. Incorporating rhythm, rhymes, and songs into exercises makes therapy more engaging and less stressful. Music stimulates the frontal lobe and limbic system to translate information throughout the mammal and cortex. Various combinations of stimuli delivered to the sensory systems engage the brain connections to accept and interpret information. When these types of therapy techniques are used in play, the baby stays happily attentive, and therapy becomes fun for both the child and the parent.

This book is designed for clinicians to use and incorporate activities with patients and caregivers. The signs and symptoms of potential challenges to the early neurological development of children are detailed. Included in this book are easy-to-follow tests for evaluating and assessing areas of delays, understanding the parts of the brain involved, and identifying the areas available for new connections for increased function, development, and progress of the child's nervous system. Exercises that can be performed at home by the patient's parent/caregiver are also included.

After receiving requests for a book from therapists, early interventionists, and parents, I have expanded my original booklet—*Ten Fingers and Ten Toes: Twenty Activities Everyone Needs to Know*—by including new information, exercises, and offering it for wider circulation. In this book, I share insider secrets from my background as a physical therapist with over forty years of experience, thirty-five of which have been dedicated to pioneering the advancement and availability of early intervention programs for infants with and without disabilities.

This program was developed by integrating information gained from a self-funded ten-year successful clinical study. It was based on results of neuroplasticity techniques with parents in the home setting. This book will help you with your work with children at home or in the clinic. We are constantly developing techniques focused for particular central nervous system challenges. Here, I am sharing the introduction to the hands-on therapy to accelerate neuroplasticity in children. This is one of a conglomerate of therapy programs for which I received the President's Volunteer Service Award in 2010 from President Obama.

When I had my children, there was no operating manual on childhood development and what to do if developmental milestones were not met. Hopefully, this book will help begin to fill that need. When knowledge, skills, and understanding were given to caregivers, childcare centers, and other providers, the children in my clinic's care experienced accelerated development. By expressing interest in this program, you have taken the first, most important step in saving a child's developmental life. When I purchased a new washer and dryer, instructions were enclosed as well as a guarantee that the equipment would function as promised. Caretakers of infants and children should have at least as much guidance! This book's mission is to help provide just that—instructions for the accelerated development of the infants and children in your care.

If you feel that something *could* be done for a child, something *can* be done for that child. The neuroplasticity program I've developed relies on the partnership between therapists and caregivers to rewire the young and pliant brain of a child. The documented case study evidence presented within this curriculum will give you the support and new tools necessary to treat the children in your care. Not only *can* something be done to help children with developmental challenges, something *is* being done daily, hourly, and by the minute in clinics and homes. With this program, every child has the potential to gain additional motor skills, and you will be able to determine if the child is gaining function or losing abilities.

It is time we begin to emerge on our own as a civilized nation from the cocoon that offers delayed children and their frantic caregivers the phrase, "Wait and see." When you've reached the point where you say, "Wait and see is not for me," then you've reached the point of an open mind to learning about options that work. That's where we start.

You are many. You are the village. And, as they say, it takes a village to raise a child. In this case, it takes a village to change a child's developmental progress. Most of my patients have had neurological impairments as well as physical delays in development, so I've spent most of my physical therapy career developing techniques that work to progress development and rewire the brain. Treating the root causes of these delays reduces symptoms and allows the patient to progress more rapidly.

Sarah's Story

Sarah came into my care at three months old, diagnosed with DiGeorge Syndrome. She presented with low tone, severe torticollis, bilateral neck webbing, and was profoundly hard of hearing. She wore bilateral hearing aids and had undergone a balloon heart catheterization. Sarah's family had been given the diagnoses and had an idea of some of the challenges her conditions would present.

The feeling of being overwhelmed is common when parents receive news of this nature; some patients' families are in "fight or flight" for up to a year after receiving news that their baby has challenges and will need special care. It is difficult for family members to learn exercises when in such a fight or flight mode. Because of this, therapists should encourage multiple learning avenues for the home exercise program such as exercise pictures, videos of exercises with the child on their phone or computer, practice sessions, and teach-back opportunities.

When I arrived at Sarah's family's home, I introduced myself and immediately began an evaluation and neuroplasticity program. I began to address her specific needs, including vision, hearing, and vestibular exercises, and rotation and stimulation of her skin and joints in a three-dimensional fashion with brushing and rubbing. Within 6 weeks Sarah began to move her arms and legs to assist in rolling. Her eyes followed lights as I carried them across in front of her. Exercises combining vision and hearing while tracking objects moving in three dimensions showed increased range of motion of her cervical spine. Little Sarah showed great potential.

Because the brain remembers whatever is done the longest, before I left Sarah and her family each session, I instructed the family on how to continue the exercises at home. I explained to them how the exercises utilized neuroplasticity and how each exercise was relevant to Sarah's condition. Every member of Sarah's family was enthusiastically compliant with her exercise program and followed through with the treatment plan daily.

A year and a half after my initial visit, Sarah's mother greeted me at the door to the clinic with Sarah's hearing aids in her hand. I asked her, "Why are Sarah's hearing aids not in her ears? We need to start our therapy treatment."

She asked me to sit down because she had news that was shocking and that she did not understand. The mother said that after Sarah's hearing evaluation, the audiologist leaned forward on their chair and said they did not know what happened, but Sarah's hearing was now completely normal and there was no need for hearing aids any longer. Then they placed the child's hearing aids in her mother's hand. Sarah's neuroplasticity treatments seemed to have supported rewired hearing along with accelerating motor skills.

Neuroplasticity
and the Brain

Sometimes the biggest changes happen in small ways. Motor skills and milestones are accomplished via multiple minute neurological building blocks. As a therapist, I came to realize that if high or low tone were not in the way of a child's voluntary movement, that child would accelerate function. A love of neuroanatomy and neurophysiology as they relate to function is helpful.

When therapists understand that the underlying causes of tone are directed by neurological pathways, relevant treatment techniques are more readily discernable. Let's look at the child who experiences a cortex stroke involving a parietal lobe for instance. The stroke damages cortical areas, which in turn means those areas are not relaying sensory and motor information effectively or at all. So the lower layers of the central nervous system show up for work. The primitive reflex patterns in those lower layers may be demonstrated in response to various sensory stimuli, such as eye movements, head and neck movements, loud sounds, and changes in body position with relation to gravity. Since the primitive reflex patterns live adjacent to each other around the lower brain centers in a "gang-like manner," they are stronger together. Many times primitive reflexes are seen as not purely Asymmetrical Tonic Neck or Tonic Labyrinthine patterns. Many of the primitive reflexes are demonstrated at once and overlay each other. Those primitive reflexes appear as a result of sensation detection and usually display high tone. Vision is neurologically connecting to over 80 percent of the central nervous system. We found profound ways to "treat and retreat" primitive reflex patterns by having the eyes look the opposite direction of the primary reflex pattern.

Since tone lives in lower brain centers, the practitioner must address high or low tone specifically to progress to voluntary and purposeful movements. Sensation treatments are key to changing how the brain interprets information. Specific sensory treatment techniques free the patient from bonds of low or high tone. All skills are wired through intricate pathways within the central and peripheral nervous system. When higher cortical connections are in place and utilized for purposeful voluntary movements, the lower primitive reflexes are placed in the background. When this occurs, high tone also diminishes and may only reappear under conditions of stress, such as fever, hunger, noisy environments, and difficulty with tasks like running.

The central nervous system is made up of the brain and spinal cord. The connections within the central nervous system are stimulated and fed by use. When these connections are not used, they starve and are pruned.

Each part of the body is connected through a series of nerves and cellular communication to the spinal cord and brain. The brain uses a great deal of energy to receive, synthesize information, and tell the body how to move and function. Therefore, if a connection is not needed, the brain prunes that specific pathway to conserve energy. Neuroplasticity can be used to build or prune connections in the central nervous system, speed up the functional development of those connections, increase motor skills, and meet milestones.

Neuroplasticity happens constantly with or without awareness of the practitioner or the patient. It is my goal to assist therapists in understanding, learning, and intentionally using neuroplasticity techniques. Specific techniques assist the child in building positive and functional neurological connections. Nervous system relays are the basis upon which motor milestones are built. The nervous system dictates what the body is able to do, not the other way around. One cannot continue to move a child in and out of a sitting position, for instance, and hope that the positioning will "take."

Therapists are challenged to assist children's bodies in making new neural connections to help develop pathways for motor tasks like coming to sitting. Intentional neuroplasticity exercises forges pathways to decrease reliance on primitive reflexes and increase connections to higher centers of the central brain structures as well as the cortex. The vast majority of the children we treat have neurological involvement that is reflected in the way their bodies move or are restricted. If the neurological components of their developmental delays are treated, their symptoms change in a positive manner faster than if we managed the symptoms alone.

Therapists generally agree that neuroplasticity is a viable tool but realize they need additional teaching and training to further understand the principles of brain rewiring and to learn how to incorporate neuroplasticity into their practice. The development of advanced medical tests, genetics, CT, MRI, and fMRI scans can play a key role in addressing areas of concern and pathways for patients' potential development and rewiring.

In order to connect symptoms to treatment, therapists must have a ready understanding of anatomy, physiology, neuroanatomy, and neurophysiology. Once the therapist gains a thorough understanding of the nervous system as it relates to "how to" function, disability, tone, and primitive reflexes interaction, they are then ready to design activities to rewire function and may utilize neuroplasticity techniques daily.

COMPASS

COMPASS, my neuroplasticity program, offers tools and techniques to integrate neurological systems with patients who have restricted use of their bodies. COMPASS incorporates exercises that assist with arm and leg function without costing an arm and a leg. It is a neuroplasticity treatment system that changes brain connections through sensory intervention and rewires ever-changing motor responses.

Management of unwanted movements or tone can be achieved through the following:

1. **Neuroplasticity techniques.**

   Pro: The brain rewires connections and integrates information. Treatments are targeted at addressing lower brain levels and function to prepare the nervous system to make new pathways and implement functional motion as a result. Neuroplasticity techniques assist in making tone more typical, low or high. Neuroplasticity techniques can also reduce and resolve tremors as well as nystagmus. Vision neuroplasticity is incorporated into treatment programs for more control of eye movement and eye teaming.

   Con: None known

2. **Splinting: coverage of hand or foot.**

   Pro: Holds body part in position approximating
   typical position.

   Con: Hands and feet need to process and interpret
   sensation in order to integrate function and develop skills;
   covering them eliminates sensation experiences.

   Suggestion: If splinting is required, use an on/off
   approach. The brain remembers whatever it does
   the longest.

3. **Positioning equipment.** Use of a stander or walker is
   incorporated into therapy.

   Pro: The child looks like they are standing when parts of
   their body are supported.

   Con: Head, neck, and trunk control are essential to
   the ability to maintain standing position. Fatigue is
   common in a "stander," and equipment has no feelings.
   Be observant of the child's tolerance of supporting
   equipment. Walkers restrict rotation of trunk and arms,
   which negatively affects balance potential.

Medications to reduce spasticity are available; however, they may produce paralytic symptoms and/or reduce sensation and treat the symptom rather than the cause. I recommend neuroplasticity techniques as a first course of treatment. The central nervous system learns through sensation. When anti-spasmodic medications interfere with the sensory pathways of learning, they are interfering with neuroplasticity, which relies on sensation to promote motor skills and rerouting of neural pathways,

We may think we learn through sensory and motor functions, but it is mainly sensory in nature. Please follow this path of analysis: When sensation enters the cranial nerves and peripheral nervous system, it travels to the central nervous system for interpretation.

Outgoing information from the central nervous system determines motor performance. After the motor response, feedback loops from sensation are received. These processes assist in correcting motor activity for successful function and are again relayed in the sensory nervous system for additional feedback. Coordination of sensation information from proprioceptors, cranial nerves (balance, vision) determine the outgoing motor information which can be corrected or altered.

Learning comes through sensation; this is what we have power over. When a therapist works with a child in sitting position and moves an arm to "catch," it educates in protective responses, the patient picks up the instruction through sensory pathways. If we want to alter motor skills and attain a milestone, we must change how we deliver sensory input.

"Management" of spasticity or low tone is not the same as utilization of positive neuroplasticity rewiring techniques. Often, management of abnormal symptoms will not affect the root cause of the infirmity. Neuroplasticity, however, changes the wiring relationships of the abnormalities between involved and uninvolved areas in the central nervous system. This allows that function and motion of the body to become more attainable for the patient.

The techniques used in neuroplasticity reach multiple lobes of the brain as well as its lower centers—below and beyond the level of the lesion. When the higher brain centers are injured, the lower centers become more active. This is one of the key reasons that postures resembling primitive reflexes appear and persist after brain injuries and also why addressing the lower brain centers is essential to healing and rewiring.

The lower brain centers act as switching stations, and layers of connections can be structured so that the relay systems within the nervous system function more efficiently. The primitive reflexes have the ability to be integrated and diminish in appearance. Abnormal tone qualities can be addressed with specialized techniques that make the tone more typical or normalized. With normalized tone, motor milestones are more easily accomplished. These lower centers will then connect to the higher centers to change voluntary movement and function.

In Jason's case, a pediatric neuro-ophthalmologist at a hospital in Nashville had diagnosed him as blind at birth due to cortical vision impairment. His eyes did not work together, and for months he was unable to track with either eye. Eight months after placing Jason in our clinical program, however, his mother walked across the treatment room and her son's left eye followed her. I asked her to cross the room again without making a sound. As she crossed, his left eye followed her again. I asked if Jason's family could obtain a horse to stimulate balance for him in sitting.

As in the first clinical case, Jason had full caregiver support. Based on Jason's previous success with nontraditional therapy methods, his family bought three horses. We were all excited about the possibilities and continued intense vision and vestibular rehabilitative therapy. Within the next eight months, Jason's right eye began to follow objects and tracked in unison with the left eye. The tone in the upper extremities that had previously demonstrated spasticity became normalized and typical. He was able to look on an activity table and see (sight) a piece of food, make sense of what he saw (vision), reach, grasp, and bring it to his mouth. He loved French fries.

While sight is a powerful sense, vision is the ability to interpret what is seen. It is important to address the connection between vision and balance because we rely on these senses to increase control of motor functions in upright postures. The world is a friendlier place if one can both see and interpret what is around them. You can help increase these sensory abilities with your patients using neuroplasticity techniques.

Without stimulation, exposure, and encouragement, the unused pathways in the brain are abandoned and become nonfunctional. Progress can regress unless new and interesting activities are introduced to the child. These novel activities don't necessarily need to be as elaborate or expensive as Jason's horses, but they must be interesting and engaging for the child and the caregiver. New items in the environment combined with lively or soothing music can help information connect in the mind and body, accelerating learning and development. The worst thing a person can do in therapy is to induce boredom with ritualistic and repetitive treatment sessions, as this will accelerate the pruning of nervous system pathways.

This brings up the idea of splinting. Splints cover sensory endings that transfer information to the brain about the child's spatial position. Some splinting is necessary, as in the case of clubfeet, spina bifida, tibial torsion, and congenital deviation of finger or toe alignment. In many other situations, however, splinting may impede function by encouraging the pruning of nervous system pathways relating to sensation perception and the splinted limb. Many children wear splints for a seven-hour school day. That is a significant amount of their awake and conscious day. The brain remembers whatever it does the longest. So, what do we want their brain to remember? The feel of toys and the floor?

Think of how long an orthopedist places a cast on an arm or leg for a wrist or an ankle fracture. They know through research to remove a cast as soon as the bones are healed so that their patient may then transition to a soft support and possibly therapy. Why would a splint be much different to the limb and brain?

Since the brain is efficient and prunes connections that are not utilized, it is important to transition to neuroplasticity techniques or a soft support as soon as possible so the body does not forget that it has an arm or leg and atrophy or lose muscular function in that limb. When the brain is not allowed to receive neurosensory stimulation and firing of synapses, connections are not fed and will die off. In such cases, the brain thinks the neural connections relating to the splinted limb are no longer needed because it is not receiving stimulation related to that limb. An alternative is to brace at night for positioning especially if spasticity is present. When the child is asleep, high tone is decreased, splints find less resistance to positioning.

I treated a patient who had experienced a stroke at birth. He had been a patient of mine since he was a baby. With therapy, he progressed nicely and was able to use bilateral hands in activities and could walk, run, hop, tap his foot, and climb a slide. He then went to a school where the therapist's policy was "If there is a diagnosis of cerebral vascular accident, brace it for safety." Under the guidance of the school's therapist, he was braced for four months. When I removed the ankle-foot orthosis (AFO), he demonstrated acquired foot drop. After five months of therapy, we were still working to regain lost function. It took nine months to regain dorsiflexion in the affected lower extremity and re-pattern gait without limping. If it isn't broken….you know the saying.

In your therapy practice, do you want to manage symptoms or rewire the brain for improved function or both? Where is the line, what is the percent of delayed development, and in what areas, that will justify therapeutic care for a child? Basic physical movement precedes other more complex aspects of development such as feeding oneself and handwriting. Infants and children who receive therapeutic treatments have an easier time acquiring skills that are required to be successful in school and life.

Parental guidance led by therapists, early interventionists, and childcare providers is key in unwinding the maze of early childhood care. If a parent or physician believes there is a delay in milestones or function, there is. Please start treatment; do not wait and see. The deficiencies may be harder to treat at a later date due to altered pathway formation to accommodate altered function in the child. Remember, we are trying to connect to viable places in the central nervous system. Combining two or more sensory-motor experiences will render new and successful connections, change muscle tone, decrease tremors, and increase function.

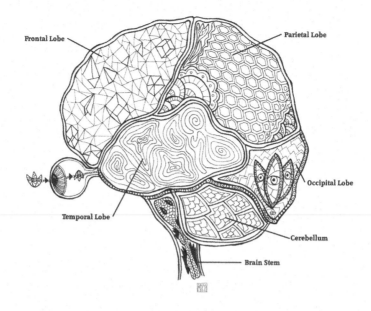

© Mica Foster DC

Brain stem – Homeostasis, reptilian brain with poor rotation abilities

Cerebellum – Responsible for smooth movements, still primitive in nature

Occipital lobe – Responsible for sight and vision, makes sense of what is seen, vision connects to 80% of central nervous system

Temporal lobe – Processes memories; integrates with taste, sight and touch, hearing, language, balance, location

Parietal lobe – Receives sensation for processing; sends out motor responses

Frontal lobe – Emotional and cognitive components for processing voluntary movements

Jordan's Story

When Jordan began therapy, he had cerebral ataxia—which caused abnormal involuntary movements—categorized as cerebral palsy, which affected his neck, trunk, bilateral arms, and legs. On Jordan's first visit, his mother said, "My baby's legs are so strong that I can't change his diaper by myself!"

I explained to Jordan's mother that Jordan's legs were perfectly normal and that what she was encountering was spasticity driven by his brain. His legs were perfect in every way, but the messages received from his brain were not correct. He had a stroke at birth which affected his trunk, arms and legs to make them feel tight. We needed to rewire his brain so that his arms and legs would get the appropriate information for coordinated motion.

When the brain suffers a bleed or injury of specific cortical layers, or when those layers suffer any damage, they function poorly or not at all, and the next central nervous system layer below the injury shows up for function. The midbrain and brainstem then begin to demonstrate more immature neurological relay actions. Primitive reflexes are demonstrated as well as changes in tone. The brain "strives to survive" and uses as much of the brain as is available.

Jordan's mother and father were instructed in exercises for daily home use. For each treatment, the exercises and activities were updated to correspond to Jordan's level of improvement or lack thereof. When Jordan started going to a childcare center, all his teachers were instructed in basic nervous system anatomy and his neuroplasticity program. We found that if caregivers have an understanding of what is driving symptoms, they feel more confident and qualified to do the exercises. Caregivers also relayed that when they understood the reason to work on activities at home, they did. As Jordan began attending grade school, each of his teachers received instruction in activities that would enhance nervous system connections and continue to progress his skills.

Progress with Neuroplasticity takes a team, and we took the time to teach his team members, to explain to them why the exercises work and how to incorporate them into his day-to-day life. Novel experiences are also very important in building multiple connections for rewiring function. When there are multiple caregivers involved, novelty is easy. Everyone has their own environment, toys and methods to carry out the home exercises.

Jordan was treated for six years. With neuroplasticity techniques, we changed how his neurons connected around neurological damage and reacted in his nervous system. Neuroplasticity built new connections and released the need for primitive reflexes, which then receded back into the background. The reticular formation monitored tone, and working through sensory directed stimulation techniques reduced the spastic tone that arrested Jordan's movements. By the end of the sixth year of treatment, this child whose legs had presented with severe spasticity, was able to walk, run, play kickball, catch a ball, write, and color with his peers without assistive devices. If we can help a child with these techniques, then these techniques will also work for you.

In addition, despite his diagnosis, Jordan did not require any assistive devices or splints—no wheelchairs or AFOs. AFOs for a child of Jordan's age typically cost $1,600 per pair in Tennessee. If Jordan had been refitted with orthotics every six months to account for his growth, the twelve pairs of AFOs he would have used over his six years of treatment would have cost over $20,000. And if Jordan had also required wheelchairs, as some children with similar diagnoses and symptoms do, the minimum cost would have been an additional $5,000 to $10,000 for each chair.

In Jordan's case, AFOs and other external devices would only have treated the symptoms of his cerebral palsy disorder. The foot and ankle are made up of 26 bones, 33 joints, more than one hundred ligaments, tendons, and muscles that respond to multidirectional stressors with use. When the foot/ankle are splinted, the forces usually received during weight-bearing, stepping, and movements are redirected—away from proprioceptors instead of toward them as is normally the case. When AFOs are removed after years of wear, foot slap, floppy ankle, and poor responses to weight shifting are demonstrated.

It's not unusual for children who wear splints while in school to have them applied early in the morning and removed sometime that evening. That is most of their "awake" day. If splints are necessary in specific cases, an **"on-off"** approach is ideal. Otherwise, connections are pruned because the brain relates to covered body parts the same as it does to body parts encased in rigid or stiff supports—it does not allow the sensors to receive information. If you don't use it, you will lose it, as needed connections will be pruned. If you want to keep connections in the central nervous system, your body must continue to fire synapses in those pathways.

In our patient population, the referrals we receive on children two-and-a-half to eight years old who previously used ankle/foot orthosis for daily constant use demonstrated disuse atrophy and weakness in the lower extremity musculature; joint laxity because the muscles and ligaments did not receive "stressors" compression; and distraction forces because of the overriding work of the brace. Weight shifting within a brace differs from barefoot or in a shoe and with removal of the brace children demonstrated insecure balance. The wearer of the brace must then be rehabilitated to a functional gait pattern. We have found that the longer the limb (and thereby also the brain) has been braced, the longer it takes to restore function.

Our goal is to rewire the brain so the *cause* of the disorder is treated. Neuroplasticity techniques treat the neurological function and connections in the nervous system, which is where the cause of the challenges reside. When the brain changes, the symptoms change. Neuroplasticity allows the brain to change how it connects and delivers the information necessary for reliable voluntary motor function.

Structure of Therapy

Evaluation

Countless families are placed into therapy programs through clinical assessments that leave them with confusing information. While we often get our first look at a child's development through charts or medical imaging, a deep neurological evaluation of the child is of key importance. It may take a few hours and more than one treatment session to adequately determine how well each of the child's senses functions and relays into the nervous system. It is equally important to see how the child responds to sensory stimulation and positional changes. Once the full picture is obtained, a therapist can develop a neurological rewiring program specific to the child.

Remember, you never step into the same nervous system twice. Like a river, a child's brain is constantly changing, developing, and learning. Frequent evaluations of a child's progress and symptoms are needed to understand their neurological development and are important to progress sensory interpretation, motor response, and skill attainment.

Your previous experience with a patient will help you determine if the therapy is working or not. If it is not working, stop doing it; it probably will not work tomorrow, either. We only have a limited time with our patients and want to progress them as expediently as we can. Try new skills and incorporate knowledge of the basis for the impairments. Neurological overviews of the cause will give you insight into how you can do this. The change of function will happen right before your eyes.

Mobility and Exercises

In my clinic, we get everyone moving from the beginning. During the evaluation process, we assess cranial nerves, lobes of the cortex and peripheral nervous system, primitive reflex patterns, tone, and milestone attainment. Then we discuss results of testing and medical history with the caregivers. We assist the parents in understanding what is working well and what is not working well to help educate and empower parents. This forms the baseline of the child's therapy program. Next, we show the caregiver how to do each activity and corresponding movements with the child, practicing to promote effectiveness. This is why each patient must be given adequate time for practice and therapy.

Each caregiver is given instructions, demonstration, practice, and video on their phone of themselves doing the exercises with feedback, coaching, and review. We refer to this practice as the *PT Phone Home* program. Through this program, the caregiver has access to their very own mentor while at home.

Using information from the caregiver's cellphone, we provide verbal instruction to clarify how to correctly perform the activity. After a few weeks or months, we view videos of the exercises with the child's caregiver to demonstrate the progress that the child has achieved. We video in regular speed and slow motion so analysis is easier; for example, the heel-toe gait.

Therapy is fun when it is incorporated into play, so the patient and their parent are encouraged to engage in play with purpose. Without a joyful and happy setting for therapy, the progress of the child can be inhibited. If a child is stressed, their mind can engage its fight-or-flight response, and the child will then be unable to learn. This fight-or-flight response can be triggered any time the child experiences fear or anxiety. Music can be used to calm or excite when connected to the therapy sessions. Music activates the limbic system, and all of the lobes in the cortex connect to it. This added music in turn also opens pathways for combining new neural connections.

If the clinic or school is loud and chaotic, or even if the lights are too bright, the child may be pushed into fight-or-flight mode, making therapy counterproductive. When a child's mind shifts into survival mode, it becomes difficult for that child to remember instructions, making it nearly impossible for them to learn and acquire new skills, or for their brain to rewire for increased neuroplasticity and functions.

Therapy exercises are child's play when they take place in a relaxing environment and are engaging and enjoyable. When the child's days are filled with purposeful movements and sensations to increase their abilities, everyone wins. Rhyming words and songs with exercises also engage multiple pathways in the central nervous system.

Goals and Results

Goals are needed from the beginning; having a clear vision for yourself and the child is of paramount importance. How can a person know where they are going if they don't know where they want to end up? We cannot motivate someone, but we can agree on common goals and let a person motivate themselves. At the start of a new therapy program, talk with the child's caregivers to find out what goals they have in mind. After hearing what they hope to accomplish, you can formulate additional goals based on the child's evaluation.

Explaining the steps necessary to accomplish larger goals will help the caregiver understand that it's not all about seeing a child immediately walking. There are nervous system connections that relay skills that are required to support motion before walking. If the child is unable to perform one or two of the connected movements or neural relays, the desired activity will be much more difficult to achieve. If the root connections and the basis for neurological function are attended to through movement, sensation, and deeper brain stimulation, then cross connections become functional and the activities will be successful.

The body develops head, neck, trunk, arms, and then the legs. Active movement of eyes, neck, trunk, and upper and lower extremities work together to accomplish rolling over; and coming to a sitting position. These are all precursors to walking. Setting realistic goals within the context of the child's development is necessary for keeping everyone engaged in therapy.

If the exercises and procedures are *administered as directed, positive results are to be expected.* Documentation and studies abound on the subject of the plasticity of the young mind. When a child's brain is fully engaged in its own connection processes, the results can be amazing. Remember to video before treatment is given so you can more easily observe the results. Keep the videos on file so the caregivers can reference before and after over various periods of time.

Education

We are all educators in some fashion or another. While working with their child, many caregivers will find themselves needing to enlighten those around them about the exercises they are doing and why the exercises are so important. Likewise, it is crucial for those of us involved in each case to fully educate caregivers as well as colleagues and the public at large about the therapeutic process.

The brain is the part of the body that is capable of interacting with interdependent systems. Experience, whether random or guided by a therapist, can wire together feelings, thoughts, sensations, and muscle actions that are then embedded in the network of brain connections. Working with two or more functions simultaneously— such as hearing and vision—connects those systems. These ideas are foundational concepts of neuroplasticity.

Nicole's story

Nicole was born six weeks early. She spent the first eight weeks of her life in the neonatal intensive care unit (NICU). She had a cleft palate, hydrocephalus, compression of the brain, ventricular septal defect, abnormalities of the spine, preterm infant muscular weakness, tethered cord in cervical and lumbar areas, Budd-Chiari syndrome, and post laminectomy syndrome of the cervical and lumbar region. She had a shunt and a feeding tube.

At five months old, Nicole's first visit from me was far from the first evaluation she had received. Her mother was overwhelmed with the news from all of Nicole's previous healthcare practitioners. "Your baby will not be able to do anything," they had stated. "We wish you the best," they would say as Mom ushered them out the door.

I introduced Nicole's mother to the concept of neuroplasticity and told her that if she worked daily with Nicole on these activities, her daughter would reach her peak potential. Nicole's mother was eager to learn and begin helping her daughter. She felt hope and the ability to set goals.

Initially, Nicole demonstrated poor head and neck control, wry neck, rounded shoulders, scapular asymmetry, muscular asymmetry, decreased thoracic kyphosis, increased lumbar lordosis, decreased cervical lordosis, and a tissue mass on the left side of her neck. She was unable to move her arms and legs against gravity in the supine position. She showed difficulty moving her head and neck left and right, which restricted the ability to turn over. This would later challenge Nicole's ability to balance in an upright posture because of poor trunk rotation. I informed Mom the sooner we could begin therapy, the better her brain would be able to rewire and improve motor skills and she agreed.

Our first exercises were visual and auditory tracking, as the eyes lead the head. Vestibular exercises with sound soon followed. With what little trunk motion Nicole was capable of, she worked hard to turn over from supine to prone. We worked on tummy time, pushing up on hands and knees then pulling up to stand, walk, and run.

When Nicole turned three, her mother was recommended by the early intervention program, to take her for testing for free pre-kindergarten based on all her diagnoses. The early intervention system thought she would surely qualify. The school's physical therapist, occupational therapist, speech therapist, and psychologist were all in attendance for Nicole's testing. Nicole's mother walked into the testing room with Nicole walking by her side, holding her hand. The school physical therapist asked where Nicole was.

"Why do you ask?" Nicole's mother asked.

"We expected Nicole to be in a wheelchair. Is she outside in the hall?"

Nicole's mother waved Nicole's hand at the physical therapist. "This is Nicole."

"That is amazing with all of her diagnostic history!" said the physical therapist. "We will begin testing now. We will probably be done in about fifteen minutes, if you'd like to wait in the hall."

Two hours later, the testers requested that Nicole be taken home. They were exhausted. "Nicole does not qualify for free pre-kindergarten. She is entirely too advanced," they told her. "Bring her back next year. She will be able to attend regular kindergarten." And so she did.

The Brain Train

The brain develops in a sequence. Like loading cars on a train, each "car" will be loaded individually then connected in sequence. Some cars are not able to carry loads of information, so adjacent cars will be used to contain the functions and information to move the child forward in development. Many times the child's body is perfectly normal, but the brain demonstrates challenges.

Lower centers of the central nervous system are the first to develop. They lay the foundation for primitive functions, such as breathing, heart beating, blood pressure regulation, eye movement, sucking, swallowing, and smelling. Initially we see reflex movements in the baby. As the baby grows and develops, these reflexes recede into the background to make way for more complex movements to emerge in the older child as the nervous system connections grow, develop, and branch to areas of the brain. If the nervous system is attended to at an early age (before ten years old), plasticity of the nervous system allows faster rewiring, restructuring, and development of the nervous system. This promotes the child's ability to receive sensory information and for that information to be interpreted and result in an appropriate motor response.

The pediatric brain is vastly different from—in many aspects—an adult brain. Its elasticity is immense, meaning that it can adapt, shift, change, and reroute multiple forms of information that it encounters and produces. This characteristic is what allows the neuroplasticity technique to work especially well in children under the age of ten, and even more so in infants and toddlers. Neuroplasticity also works for older individuals although may take longer.

Children develop active movements from the eyes and head down to the neck, trunk, arms, and then legs. The brain itself develops back to front, with the frontal lobe maturing last. This is one reason we use emotion for frontal lobe stimulation rather than executive decision-making.

Lower centers of the brain initially develop the foundation of primitive movements and functions. This includes movement of the eyes following an object, mouth sucking, swallowing, hearing, and primitive balance of the head and neck to hold itself upright, as well as movement of the arms and legs. Some of the movements we see in a baby are reflex type (e.g., their hand gripping your finger). These reflexes give way to more complicated movements by the time the baby reaches the age of six to twelve months (e.g., they can grip a toy and release it).

The nervous system connections grow, develop, and branch to areas of the brain and various parts of the nervous system. When the functional areas of the central nervous system are treated, it allows the plastic nature of neural systems to connect to mammal brain and cortex to promote functional developmental milestones. The nervous system sorts information for retrieval rather than allowing sensory overload or confusion to the child. Deliver activities that follow the same pattern as the neurological system's development sequence. This makes it easier for the brain to use it's own filing systems, to make sense of sensation, then accept and integrate new information for use.

Basic Neuroanatomy
of Neuroplasticity

Let's take a brief tour of the central nervous system to understand the interconnectivity, overlapping, and alternate pathways of sensory and motor function.

Neurological Development of the Central Nervous System

The basic pattern of brain formation can be seen throughout the lifetime as established in fetal development. In other words, neurological growth begins from the top—beginning with the notochord—and works its way down and out. The brain also develops from the back to the front, with frontal lobe maturing last.

By the age of two, two-thirds of the brain development has occurred. What's not yet completely developed and active at this stage is the frontal lobe; which depends on "time" relevance, reasoning and executive decision making. . One can think of the frontal lobe wearing a watch with reason, truth, and consequences. The 2-year-old child is in the "present."

During the teenage years, the brain resembles the adult brain but does not yet demonstrate mature function. By adulthood, brain growth is complete, but the brain is still constantly establishing new pathways to facilitate learning and attain new skills. This constant change allows practitioners to increase and alter pathway connections via neuroplasticity techniques in themselves and patients.

Glial cells continually develop and assist the brain in making new connections in conjunction with novel sensory experiences. This pattern of continual growth and learning allows adults to master new hobbies and sports throughout their lives. The adult brain's ability to learn and adapt is responsible for enabling a person to change careers, learn new technologies, and remember new ideas. Even as you read this book, you are expanding your own brain connections. It is my hope that this text will gift you with new eyes as your examine and treat your patients.

Brain Stem

This part of the brain sitting beneath the cerebrum in front of the cerebellum connects the brain to the spinal cord. It houses homeostasis functions such as breathing and involuntary processes like heart rate, blood pressure, and digestion. These survival processes are residents in the brain stem as well as primitive reflex movements. The brain stem is also the headquarters of tone; high and low tones originate here. Neuroplasticity treatment techniques for recalibrating tone qualities in a child must reach into the brain stem to be effective.

Brain stem: midbrain, pons, and medulla, oblongata lay underneath the limbic system

1. Joins continuously with the spinal cord.

2. Midbrain.

3. Pons.

4. Medulla oblongata.

5. Regulation of cardiac and respiratory function.

6. Ten of the twelve pairs of cranial nerves—III–XII—arise from the brain stem.

7. Assists in maintaining consciousness; alertness and awareness.

8. Provides the main motor and sensory innervation to the face.

9. Nerve connections of the motor and sensory pathways pass through the brain stem. It has a major role in neural conduction between the body to the cerebrum and cerebellum.

10. Reptilian brain: Functions in basic movements void of rotation ability. If the brain stem is damaged, the child will be unable to roll over; decreased rotation of neck, trunk, arms, and legs. Poor balance in sitting and standing, which is dependent on rotation ability.

11. Stimulation directed to cranial nerves is delivered to the brain stem instantaneously.

12. Jean-Pierre Barral and Alain Croibier in the book "Manual Therapy for the Cranial Nerves" (2009) described positive effects on the patient's nervous system through treatment of the cranial nerves. Treatment has an effect on the visceral system and sympathetic nervous system.

Cranial Nerves

I *Cranial nerve – Olfactory – extension of the brain track*

Type: Sensory

Emerges from - Cerebrum and forebrain

Function- Smell

Injury - Anosmia (no smell), distortion of smell, affects taste.

Stimulation – Smells – recommend citrus

II *Cranial nerve – Optic – extension of the brain track*

Type: Sensory

Emerges from – Forebrain, cerebrum

Function - Sight

Injury - Visual field blindness: homonymous hemianopsia (L/R), or bilateral

Hemianopsia or hemianopia visual loss on the same side of both eyes

Stimulation - Light, tracking, add sound to rewire

III Cranial nerve – Occulomotor

Type: Motor

Emerges from – Brain stem

Function – Somatic motor innervates control of 4 of the 6 eye muscles for movements and raises eyelid

Visceral motor delivers parasympathetic information for appropriate response control of pupil and lens for pupil constriction and accommodation

Injury - Double vision (diplopia), unable to coordinate movement of both eyes (strabismus), eyelid dropping (ptosis), or eyelid paralysis; may have accommodating head tilt to reduce symptoms.

Stimulation – Light stimulation one or both eyes, manual therapy to eyebrow and eyelid.

IV Cranial nerve - Trochlear

Type: Motor

Emerges from - dorsal aspect of brainstem – Only cranial nerve that innervates muscle on the opposite side from its origin

Function – Eye movement directed by the superior oblique muscle. Primary action is medial rotation or intorsion. Secondary actions are adduction and inferior rotation of eye. The tertiary action is abduction, movement away from midline.

Injury – Eye drifts up and medial, patient tilts head to opposite side and forward.

May tuck chin in to merge 2 visual fields – torsional diplopia

Stimulation – Visual tracking up and down, medial and lateral. Treat with increased emphasis on down and medial paired with vestibulocochlear stimulation – sound plus rock, roll and swing motions.

V Cranial nerve - Trigeminal

Type: Motor and Sensory

Emerges from – Brainstem – each side of the pons - 3 branches – ophthalmic (S), maxillary (S), Mandibular (S & M),

Function – Brachial Motor controls muscles of the face and functions such as biting and chewing.

Somatic Sensory receives sensation from the face.

Injury – With impingement of cranial nerve, jaw will deviate toward paralyzed side when mouth opened

Stimulation – Cool, manual rub, vibration (not around the lips) or use of small electric stimulation

VI Cranial nerve – Abducens

Type: Motor

Emerges from - Brainstem

Function – Eye movement, lateral rectus muscle, brings the cyc away from midline

Injury – Reduced lateral movement of eye

Stimulation – Vision tracking combined with hearing. Rock, roll and swing.

VII Cranial nerve – Facial

Type: Motor and Sensory

Emerges from - Brainstem

Function – Branchial motor branch provides muscular control of face, facial expressions, examine symmetry of face, eyebrows, cheek tone

Somatic sensory receives taste sensation from the front of the tongue.

Injury – Drooping of eyebrow and of the mouth, difficulty chewing and sucking bottle.

Stimulation – Manual, myofascial release to face. Muscles of the face produce rotation movements.

VIII Cranial nerve – Vestibulocochlear

Type: Special Sensory

Emerges from - brainstem

Function – Hearing and balance. There are 2 nerve branches. The vestibular track assists in equilibrium functions. Cochlear or acoustic nerve is responsible for auditory information to be relayed to the brain.

Vestibuloocular reflex keeps eyes image stable when head moves during activities.

Injury – Vestibular: Dizziness, difficulty maintaining upright posture. Cochlear: Insufficient hearing full spectrum of sound to deafness.

Stimulation - Rock, roll and swing. Visual tracking. Combine hearing and vision stimulation.

IX Cranial nerve - Glossopharyngeal

Type: Motor and Sensory

Emerges from - Brainstem

Function – Brachial motor – controls one of the muscles of the pharynx

Visceral motor – Parasympathetic control of the parotid salivary gland

Special sensory – Taste sensation from the back portion of the tongue

Visceral sensory – Detection of blood pressure changes

Injury - Loss of gag reflex, deviation of the uvula

Stimulation – Manual therapy delivered in oral cavity and tongue. Cool chew tubes.

X Cranial nerve - Vagus

Type: Motor and Sensory

Emerges from – Medulla oblongata

Function – Interface with parasympathetic control of internal organs of thorax and abdomen.

Damage to vagus nerve may have an affect on digestive tract function.

Visceral motor directs parasympathetic control of internal organs.

Visceral sensory receives information from the internal organs.

Brachial motor control muscles of the larynx and pharynx.

Injury – There may be a rise of blood pressure and heart rate. Patient may demonstrate a hoarse voice and difficulty swallowing.

Stimulation – Wherever you treat the patient set up a calm environment and voice. Vagus nerve and organ distribution manual treatments can also be part of the treatments.

XI Cranial nerve – Accessory

Type: Motor

Emerges from – Upper segments of the spinal cord and is the only nerve to enter and exit the skull

Function – Assists in shoulder elevation (upper portion of trapezius innervation) and head turning via the sternocleidomastoid (SCM).

Injury – Difficulty with movements of shoulder, scapula and neck. May contribute to torticollis postures.

Stimulation – Manual therapy to SCM and upper trapezius, visual tracking left and right.

XII Cranial nerve - Hypoglossal

Type: Motor

Emerges from – Innervation from bilateral hemispheres of the brain

Function – Innervates the muscles of tongue. Hypoglossal function is required for speech, food manipulation and swallowing.

Injury – Fasciculation or atrophy of one or both sides of the tongue. With tongue protrusion deviation will be toward involved side.

Stimulation – Manual therapy to masseter, temporalis, and sling muscles of lower jaw and tongue.

Damage to the Brainstem

When the brainstem is damaged, the practitioner may see effects on cranial nerves III–XII, including voice change, difficulty swallowing, hearing difficulties, and dizziness. Treatment is through the sensory pathways to rewire information. Some of these neural paths include spinothalamic, dorsal column, fasciculus gracilis, and medial lemniscus and include temperature sensation, touch, proprioception, and pressure.

Suggestion: Rewire and pair through what is working.

Brodal P. (2004).The Central Nervous System, 3rd ed. Oxford University Press.

Patten J. (1996). Neurological Differential Diagnosis, 2nd ed. Springer.

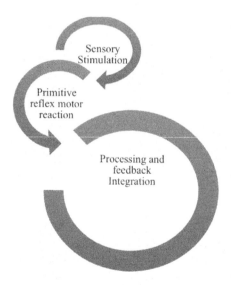

As the nervous system grows and develops, primitive reflexes are integrated. When this process of placing the primitive reflexes in the background is delayed, motor skill development is slowed and indicates neurological impairment. Exercises that promote rewiring of the nervous system will increase neurological connectivity and integration.

Williams and Shellenberge.(1996).Pyramid of Learning describes basic information entering the nervous system as development occurs and more complex activities are performed.

Information enters the nervous system through tactile, vestibular, and proprioceptive receptors.

Cranial Nerve Stimulation – *through vision, smell, taste, hearing, sensation, and more.*

Sensory information travels from the head, neck and face to then reinforce realization of where the body is, awareness of two sides of the body/extremities, postural coordination, and motor planning. A basic pyramid of activities begins in the central nervous system then extends peripherally to promote the accomplishment of advanced motor skills.

1. Eye-hand coordination has dependence on ocular-motor control

2. Visual-spatial perception, auditory/language skill/attention ability

3. Self-care, dressing, daily living activities, behavior, intellect demonstrated, academic learning, active cognition

I. **Olfactory Nerve**. The sense of smell is delivered to the nervous system via the olfactory nerve. The impulses from the olfactory nerve travel to the thalamus then to the olfactory cortex of the frontal lobe. Connections to the limbic system can elicit emotional responses. For instance, limbic system response to the smell of baking bread can evoke pleasant emotions, while the response to the smell of a skunk can elicit feelings of danger.

II. **Optic Nerve**. Vision connects to over 80 percent of the central nervous system which makes for a powerful tool in neural rewiring. The eyes constantly fix on objects whether moving or still. Visual tracking, also called smooth pursuit, is when the eyes follow toys or objects. A saccade or a jumping of the eye to fixate on one point or another, can be reflexive or an active movement. Visual skills are also active when the child is moving in their environment; it assists in maintaining an orientated picture of the child's world around them.

III. Oculomotor Nerve. The oculomotor nerve controls eye movement, raises eyelids, rotate eyes and through pupil constriction adjust the amount of light entering the eyes. Use light to stimulate one or both eyes. Damage to this nerve may cause strabismus and inability to coordinate movements of both eyes, eyelid drooping. Therapists evaluate the competency of this nerve function in accommodating torticollis positions, head tilt may be used to alleviate symptoms of eye drooping.

IV. Trochlear Nerve. The trochlear nerve is involved in eye movement. The superior oblique muscle connects to the annular tendon. The trochlear nerve processes brain signals and innervates the superior oblique eye muscle, moving the eyes up, down, and lateral. Work with light and toys for visual tracking. When adding this exercise with sound, eye movement will wire with hearing.

V. Trigeminal Nerve. The trigeminal nerve is responsible for sending and receiving somatosensory information (pain and touch) from the face, head, and muscles for chewing. Manual therapy to the face will stimulate the rotation ability of the muscles.

VI. Abducens Nerve: The abducens nerve is responsible for eye movement away from the nose via the lateral rectus muscle. Visual tracking with medial and lateral movements assists in sending information for stimulation and exercise of this pathway. This is an extremely important movement in reading and for safety in the environment for a child.

VII. Facial Nerve. The facial nerve controls the muscles used in facial expression. It receives information from taste on the anterior two-thirds of tongue and somatosensory neural information from the ear. Myofascial release and manual therapy to the face assists in stimulation of these muscles. Add scent in the room (not touching the child) such as lemon, orange, or grapefruit, and the olfactory nerve will crosswire information with facial expression.

VIII. Vestibulocochlear Nerve. The vestibular organs provide information about spatial orientation, posture in relation to gravity and movement, balance, and vision. This organ system in each ear is made up of three semicircular canals lying in different directions at right angles to each other. They provide information about starting and stopping various directional movements.

The vestibular organs also contribute information for appropriate elicitation of protective responses and maintenance of upright posture. Damage to the vestibular sensory system causes significant challenges in development. Some children will demonstrate typical protective responses. Other children may only demonstrate protective response with increased speed and an increased angle off midline.. Early treatment is imperative to reconnect the senses of orientation and balance so the child is able to advance motor skills.

The vestibulocochlear nerve communicates to the vestibular nuclei to control neck and eye movements with regard to the body's position in space. There are also connections to the thalamus and cortical regions of the brain. The vestibular nuclei are located adjacent to the fourth ventricle on the brain stem. Sometimes with hydrocephalus, pressure, or damage to any tracks along the passages to the ears, nystagmus or accommodating neck movements may occur.

The vestibular system from each side of the head contributes a group of fibers called the medial longitudinal fasciculus (MLF) toward the midline of the medulla, pons, and spinal cord. The MLF is especially important because it connects the cranial nerves with the vestibular system. The MLF is near the middle of the brain stem and has ascending (sensory) and descending (motor) fibers. It is involved in eye movement, head and neck proprioceptors, and alignment.

To visualize the inter-coordinated pathways of the central nervous system, look at the connectivity of the semicircular canal pathway. When the horizontal semicircular canal is stimulated by the head turning to the left pathway, the eyes will turn to the right to maintain fixation. The vestibular portion of VIII goes to the vestibular nuclei, which then travels to the right side of the medulla and connects to the medial longitudinal fasciculus to join in coordination of the right abducens nerve VI. When a patient looks to the right side the lateral rectus turns the right eye to the right/lateral and left oculomotor nerve III innervates the medial rectus to turn the left eye toward the nose/medial for coordinated eye movement.

IX. Glossopharyngeal Nerve. The glossopharyngeal nerve receives somatosensory input from the posterior third of tongue, tonsils, and pharynx. The glossopharyngeal nerve is helpful in swallowing. Consider if the infant/child has been intubated and the possible effects on sucking and swallowing. Try different textures, nipples on bottles, and pacifiers to assist in mouth closure for swallowing. Sensory techniques can change tone in the face of neurologically compromised patients. It is essential to make the tone in the facial muscles typical for mouth closure and the tongue to move for swallowing. Try swallowing with your mouth open.

X. Vagus Nerve. What happens in vagus does not stay in vagus. It is a long and wandering nerve and reaches the viscera—sensory, motor, and autonomic functions. Damage to the vagus nerve has far-reaching effects. Damage to the vagus nerve may demonstrate loss of parasympathetic innervation, an increase in blood pressure, heart rate, hoarse voice and difficulty swallowing.

XI. Spinal Accessory Nerve. The spinal accessory nerve assists in shoulder elevation, head turning, head and neck motor control. As therapists we need to assess this nerve and muscle function in children with Torticollis. Evaluate to see if there is winging of the scapula and weakness of the levator scapulae and sternocleidomastoid muscle.

XII. Hypoglossal Nerve. The hypoglossal nerve is responsible for tongue motor control as it assists in swallowing and allows intricate tongue movements for food manipulation and clear speech production. This nerve is unique in that it is innervated by both hemispheres of the brain, can clearly demonstrate one sided impairment of the nerve. The damage can be demonstrated by visible fasciculation of the tongue or atrophy of the tongue. Check below the tongue for lingual frenulum attachments, to see if the tongue can move freely for effective speech and swallowing.

Primitive Reflex	Stimulation	Purpose	Appearance	Integration	Persistence
Rooting	Touch cheek	Feeding	Birth	3–4 months	Thumb suck, speech, and articulation challenges
ASTNR	Eye, head turn	Assist through birth canal, develop cross-pattern moves	Birth	6 months	Difficulty with eye-hand coordination, crossing midline, visual tracking
Palmar Grasp	Touch of palmar surface	Grasp	Birth	5–6 Months	Poor Fine motor skills, difficulty letting go
Spinal Gallant	Stroke side paraspinals	Assist with birth process	Birth	3–9 Months	Postural issues
Tonic Labyrinthine	Extend or flex the neck, shoulder retraction- hip extension or opposite	Head and neck control in womb and after birth, management of postural stability	In utero	3 ½ years	Poor muscle tone, may walk on toes, spatial orientation dysfunction
Moro	Head/neck tilt in extension quickly	Defense	Birth	2–4 months	Hypersensitivity, hyper-reactivity, difficulty sitting
Landau	Lift in air prone like superman	Posture development	4–18 months	1 year	Challenged motor development
Symmetrical Tonic Neck	Neck and arms flex, legs extend	Prepare for crawling	6–9 months	9–11 months	Poor muscle tone, eye-hand coordination

Primitive reflexes are initially seen in the very young child. These reflexes stimulate the child's ability to move in response to sensory stimulation. If they are not integrated, they may act as blocks to development. This can appear as movement challenges, reading difficulties, writing difficulties, and/or language and speech delays.

I believe vision is the dominant dictator and the eyes lead the head. In years past, we were taught that head and neck turning will decrease primitive reflex elicitation. The patient needs to look before they turn. If a patient *looks* to the opposite direction of the stimulus of the primitive reflex, the power of the reflex is diminished. Active visual tracking of a toy is ideal for eye movements. Vision connects neural relay system pathways to all layers of the central nervous system.

Integration of the primitive reflexes is very important even for the visual and vestibular rehabilitation practitioners. If there is retention or obligatory primitive reflex demonstration after typical expected integration, motor function of the child will be affected.

Moro Reflex. Vestibular problems are found as well as eye and visual perceptual problems. A patient will visually explore the perimeter of a shape rather than the internal features (page), difficulty with background noise audio discrimination. It is elicited by looking up. Have the child look down at toys and give instructions from a neutral eye level.

Asymmetrical Tonic Neck Reflex. When this reflex is obligatory there is difficulty with head movements affecting balance control, visual perceptual problems, and difficulty crossing midline visually or with extremities. There are challenges with poor visual tracking and problems crossing midline. This will later negatively affect learning to read, telling time, and left-right distinctions.

Symmetrical Tonic Neck Reflex. Some symptoms are clumsiness, slowness in pencil/paper tasks, poor eye-hand coordination, slumped posture in sitting. An older child or adult may demonstrate poor posture, eye-hand coordination difficulties, and focus challenges.

Spinal Galant Reflex. Hip rotation to one side when ambulating.

Tonic Labyrinthine Reflex. Patients may demonstrate lower tone, vision and vestibular challenges, poor balance, difficulty with eye movement, difficulty with spatial orientation. These children have poor balance, orientation and physical balance.

http://www.minnesotavisiontherapy.com/retained_reflexes retrieved 071415

http://visiontherapyathome.com/ retrieved 071415

https://www.ncbi.nlm.nih.gov/pmc/articles/PMC5778413/ retrieved 082418

There are multiple tests available for assessing retained primitive reflexes past the age of expected integration. One of the tests available is MOT for children and is divided into four areas: stability, locomotion, object control, and fine movement skills. Sally Goddard also has a five-point rating scale.

Goddard-Blythe S. (200)6 The well balanced child. Warsaw: Świat Książki.

Children and adults with integrated primitive reflexes may still demonstrate them under duress. On the interstate, drivers have been instructed to move over an additional lane away from a policeman, road maintenance crew, and stalled cars. In an analogous way, when we turn our eyes, head, and neck there is increased extension on the "look side" and flexion on the "look away side." Hence, we turn our "car" into the hazard.

When paddling down a river, don't look at the rock. If you do, you will go toward the rock with your boat. Football players running for a touchdown often hold the ball in their flexed arm and reach out with their "look side" arm. Testing primitive reflex dominance is quite different from evaluating their presence. Primitive reflexes are always there. Our decision comes down to whether we need to place them further in the background into nonobligatory brain status through sensory and motor exercises.

Neuroplasticity
Combination Exercises

Why start at the top? Sensory stimulation through primary senses reaches the nervous system quickly and in an orderly and organized fashion. The information sent into the nervous system is processed quickly and determines motor skills that need to be engaged in response. The developmental organization of the fetal brain, is the same sequence we deliver sensory information into the awaiting nervous system. When we deliver sensory information and experiences to the child in this fashion, the brain can process and learn more quickly. This is because the information is organized and developmentally stacked. As a child, if we were taught the alphabet in random order, we may have never learned to read.

What is so important about routine and novel activities? The more novel the activity, the more the brain will increase alertness and bring in processing to integrate a new memory to be retrieved at a later time. Sleep is also important because the hippocampus synthesizes and organizes information during rapid eye movement (REM) sleep. It then throws memories back into the cortex for retrieval when needed. If a child has difficulty sleeping seven to nine hours, they may not be getting enough deep and REM sleep to process memories that will stick.

Matthew Walker PhD. (2018). Why We Sleep: Unlocking the Power of Sleep and Dreams.

Find Out What Is Working and What Is Not Working

Cranial nerves emerge directly from the brain and brainstem. Information that enters the sensory endings travels a very short distance to the brain to deliver information. With sensory engagement of the cranial nerves that enter the brain and brain stem directly, you will see faster results. This is where organization of developmental stacking begins to integrate information low in the central nervous system. This provides the neural network foundation for effective higher level fine and gross motor skill performance.

A study reported in the *Iranian Journal of Child Neurology* compared commonly used sensory integration and neurodevelopmental techniques relative to the improvement of gross motor function in children with cerebral palsy. The study's method significantly increased control of gross motor function, which is one of the most important goals of a therapy session. Both therapies demonstrated positive results with the developmental milestones of rolling, sitting, crawling, kneeling, and standing. There was no significant improvement in walking, running or jumping. Shamsoddini A. (2010) Comparison Between the Effect of Neurodevelopmental Treatment and Sensory Integration Therapy on Gross Motor Function in Children with Cerebral Palsy. *Iranian Journal of Child Neurology*. There are different types of sensory integration therapy which offer mixed results.

To provide optimum results in neurological rewiring we need to consider what happens in the nervous system itself. The Hebb theory in neuroscience accounts for the adaption of firing neurons during a learning process. Whatever fires together will wire together. In 1949, Donald Hebb described that repeated synapses in a response to stimulation become a learned pathway. Let us look at repeated stimulation.

Gross and fine motor movements of voluntary and purposeful functions will progressively increase if directed by a trained therapist. On the flip side, if intentional stimulation is not provided for hands, feet, touch, pressure, weight-bearing on proprioceptors, the nervous system will be confused and neglected. The child may demonstrate reliance on lower-brain-center primitive reflex patterns rather than higher-brain-center-driven voluntary movements in the midbrain and cortex because of disconnections. To help a patient progress to higher connection processing in the nervous system, the practitioner will deliver stimulation of a sensory function that is "working" with one that is not functioning well or not functioning at all. These will then fire together to wire together.

The child's knowledge of where their body is provides a basis for coordinated movements and realization of three-dimensional space, including where their body is in relation to objects. Stimulation of the head, neck, trunk, arms, and legs with a brisk rubbing fashion assists in waking up the skin sensors, and allows the mind to be aware of the body. Everything in the environment is in relation to one's own location of their body. For example, the glass of water is to the right and on the table in front of me.

Visualize a burned match; what do your senses tell you? This specific memory is common to many of us. The ability to retrieve it is made possible by the processing, organization and memory of your central nervous system. Children who experience damage to the brain, midbrain, or brainstem may have difficulties holding images as well as performing motor functions related to procedural skills requested by the therapist.

Visual tracking in X-, Y-, and Z-axis involves three-dimensional movement of the eyes: left/right, up/down, and near/far. There are additional movements, but we will start here. The motions of the eyes work the eye muscles, which can also shape the eyeball and aid in focus ability. Reading relies on left/right and up/down movements. Near/far focus assists with safety, running, ball sports, and depth perception.

Academically, we were taught that passive or active movements of the head and neck may stimulate primitive reflexes. I want to challenge that premise with this thought: the voluntary movement of the eyes are first, followed by the head and neck.

Visual tracking is one of the first movements of an infant. These changes in eye direction decrease the power of primitive reflex patterns. Movement of the eyes in the opposite direction of the elicitation of a primitive reflex will allow the therapist to move body parts so therapy and desensitization may be delivered to the trunk and extremities.

For example, sit with your face and eyes looking forward at a point on the wall. Move your face to the right but not your eyes; keep your eyes fixed on the point. This is a difficult move for some of us, whereas looking to the right with the eyes alone is usually no challenge.

Below are some of the activities we use in our clinic. In my seminars various techniques are described, delivered and practiced with before- and after-treatment videos.

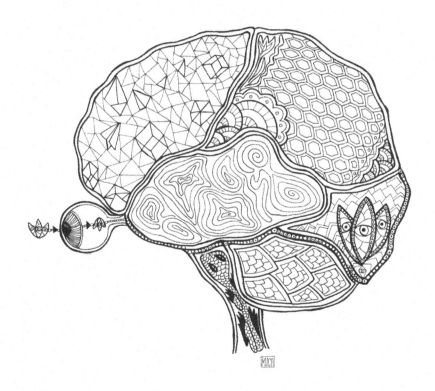

Make sense of the senses and suggestions for stimulation

Visually follow an object (listed below) and/or an emotional face up/down, left/right, near/far.

1. Hand

2. Toy

3. Light

4. Sound

5. Combination of stimulation using sounds with visual tracking; add a rattle to the light, thereby pairing vision with hearing. Remember whatever fires together – wires together.

6. **Visual tracking:** up, down, right, left, near, far – crosses midline and strengthens the eye muscles, infinity "8" crossing each side.

7. Motion – speed and direction, start slowly then increase speed

8. Determine basic field of vision

9. Face – children may be attracted to faces or toys with eyes

10. Voice – use different tone of voice

11. Emotion and Music– this can be utilized with voice tone and facial expression, slow and calming or fast and exciting, high and low tone are influenced by music

12. If a child is blind use hearing and touch on the same side for tracking

Vision chart

1. How to stimulate; use varying colors and sizes and keep it novel.

2. Determine how far the patient can focus, watch their expression and reaching for toy.

3. Use cranial nerve conduction; optic and auditory are fast conductors for treatment.

4. Combine functions: vision, sound, emotion, smell, fire together to wire together.

Hearing – move object from one location to the next

1. Left ear

2. Right ear

3. Use of location: up, down, left, right, near, and far.

4. Stimulate near and far from ear with toy sounds, rattle, and voice.

Vestibulocochlear

1. Rock, roll, swing, and balance. If the child is small, place them in your arms or the arms of the caregiver

2. Movement of the head - yes, no, tilt head side to side – ear toward shoulder.

3. If the child is larger than you can handle safely, rock the child in a swing or a blanket.

4. Slow or fast movement? Depends on what type of tone you want to stimulate.

Rocking slowly will produce sedative effects to reduce tone.

Rock fast to increase tone; may interact with fight-or-flight response.

Smell Stimulation may help make new stem cells –

Belluscio, L. (2014). Scientists sniff out unexpected role for stem cells in the brain, NIH scientists find that restocking new cells in the brain's center for smell maintain crucial circuitry.

Cummings DM. (2014). Adult neurogenesis is necessary to refine and maintain circuit specificity. *Journal of Neuroscience.*

1. Use safe smells such as blooming flowers, citrus, herbs.

2. Olfactory stimulation

3. Use smells from kitchen

4. Do not place essential oils on a child. You may place essential oils on a cotton ball in the room with caregivers' permission

5. Use novel smells; change the scent weekly

6. Have caregivers bring the child's favorite smells to treatment sessions.

Touch – use all three-dimensional touch, with both high and low tone

1. Avoid sensation around mouth and diaper regions due to the large number of receptors.

2. Tapping over muscle bellies or tendons

3. Sensory stimulation skin – quick and brisk similar to rubbing off dried sand

4. Temperature – cool only, place toys, puzzles, balls in refrigerator

5. Pressure – light or deep

6. Brushing – can be done with therapy brush or inside out sock

7. Combination – use of two or more stimulation treatments at once

8. Positional – use in integrating primitive reflexes – visually track while receiving stimulation to decrease tone since it allies with primitive reflex patterns

9. Normalize high tone – longer time of stimulation to numb and dumb.

10. Low tone qualities – make stimulation quick and brisk to wake up reactions

Vibration – handheld – best to use electric with variable speeds. Do not use the vibrator around the mouth or around the diaper area; because of the high density of nerve endings in these areas, stimulation may overload the nervous system. Tone is sensory driven and can be altered.

Vibration can act as a stimulator for a short duration over a body part. This method can also increase tone in a low-tone infant or child.

The vibrator can also decrease tone. Used for a prolonged duration, it can "numb and dumb" the arm, hand or leg and foot that demonstrates a spastic pattern. Remember that high and low tone also live in the trunk.

Benefits of Neuroplasticity techniques

1. Shorter duration of treatments

2. Home program compliance

3. Faster rewiring

4. Improved function

5. Demonstrates advanced motor skills

6. Uses videos to show progress for increased memory and compliance with program

7. Acknowledges caregivers as helping to facilitate improvements in a child's function

Types of stimulation

1. Specific stimulation

   a. It is important for the child to recognize they have a whole body and how they are oriented in space. All orientation and reference is in regard to their particular sensory location. Start sensory stimulation with the head and neck, trunk, arms then legs since this is the same way the body develops. You can then go back and stimulate specifically the arm, hand, leg, and foot areas of deep concern.

   b. Suggest therapists use multiple types of stimulation modalities

2. Use combination stimulation to wire around challenged areas of the central nervous system.

    a. Connect several senses: vision, taste, smell, and sound. Perform each individually initially then add in combination. Careful to avoid overloading their sensory abilities.

    b. The child will be able to pull information out of one of the file memories attached to the sensation, then will be able to wean from dependence of the additional sensations added to an activity. Example, cool the puzzle or pencil in the refrigerator, so the child knows the puzzle or pencil is different than themselves. Soon the item will not need cooling for the child to be able to work on tasks.

    c. Music is a connector because of emotion and the limbic system. Music on a birthday can house memories of food, smells, and how you felt.

    d. Somatic sensory acuity is related to receptive field size, peripheral innervation density, and extent of cortical representation. The more one practices an activity, the more space the parietal cortex dedicates to that activity. Parietal association cortex is also important for interpreting the "meaning" of a somatic stimulus.

Schmidt,R.(1986) *Fundamentals of Sensory Physiology*, 3rd Ed, New York: Springer-Verlag.

Exercise sequencing

Stimulate, rub all over the body (but avoid the mouth and diaper areas), wake up the nervous system, narrate parts of the body saying phrases such as "This is your head, face, neck, etc."

Tap thymus for increasing alertness and tone if needed.

Primitive reflex integration

1. Move eyes in sequence with completion of reflex pattern

2. Stimulate visual tracking opposite direction of the reflex pattern

3. Move eyes, head, and neck opposite of reflex

4. Continue tracking to move eyes farther

5. This decreases the power of spasticity in the reflex pattern

6. The therapist can then work on desensitization of the trunk, arms, hands, legs or feet

7. Fatigue the reflex pattern with stimulation, brisk rubbing of trunk, arm, and leg

8. Repeat visual tracking in and out of primitive reflex pattern after "numbing and dumbing" stimulation techniques.

9. Cool stimulation using 4 ounces of corn syrup in a quart freezer Ziploc from the refrigerator can also wake up body parts that were previously disregarded or physically neglected. Gently move the Ziploc over the areas to awaken. Do not sustain cold on an area of the child.

Tips for Common Challenges

The child commonly has difficulty with trunk rotation after abdominal surgery, heart surgery, or g-tube insertion due to scarring. Adhesions restrict rolling, come to sit, balance, pull to stand, and ambulation. Manual releasing techniques for scarring are useful for increasing the flexibility of fascia tissues to allow unrestricted movements. The therapist can also make a negative pressure pad with a one-inch foam with a cut-out over the G-tube or two-inch pad cut out over tracheostomy tubing. Velcro the pad to the child. This will divert the prone position support pressure on other non-painful areas. Once they get the skills of rolling and coming to sitting, they will move on to more advanced skills.

A technique we utilize for paresthesia and neglect on a part of the body is to simultaneously stimulate symmetrical body parts (both arms and both legs) with narration and emotion. This technique also is useful with agenesis of the corpus callosum. The brain will identify and coordinate information on its own and repair the body image to match the request of the central nervous system. For spina bifida, provide sensory stimulation from neck to toes.

ASTNR (Asymmetrical Tonic Neck Reflex) This is done as an active movement of the child. Stimulate the child to turn head to the right, hold the position, and then visually track eyes to the left followed by the head. Repeat. (The practitioner can fatigue the reflex patterns by repetition.) Add higher-level skills from the midbrain area, such as crawling, creeping, tall-kneeling combined with eyes, head, and neck rotation left and right. There are cases where the child has difficulty with head turning or visual tracking. The therapist can maintain the position by placing a rolled towel under the head to reduce rolling, then stimulate vision or hearing with light and sound to entice tracking laterally the opposite direction.

Rotation Movements start with a rotation component. The first rotation is the eyes. This is followed by head and neck and trunk; hence, rolling over is enticed by visual tracking. Rotation of upper and lower extremities initiates movements of reaching, hand-to-mouth action, balance in standing and play.

Clasped hands and indwelling thumbs treatment: desensitize hands, use ASTNR and looking down the arm will extend arm and hand as the therapist holds to the carpals and externally rotates the forearm "Numb and dumb" the flexors and palm of the hand with vibration. If splints are used to open the hand, consider keeping the palm and fingertips exposed to further integrate the palmar grasp. When the palms and fingers are covered, the stimulation opportunities are stolen from the hand, causing disuse atrophy, agnosia and pruning of connections to occur (similar to long-term cast wearing).

Initially, have the child start crawling and creeping with neutral eye targets (eye level at midline.) If eye targets are above, below, right, or left of midpoint, a primitive reflex may be elicited and interfere with active movements. Video these actions in slow motion. Move to cross-crawl patterning with stimulation of eye movement of neutral points for eye levels, then progress to moving eye targets to superior, inferior, left, and right of neutral.

If the child is toe walking. Record the child on slow motion video. Where is the visual focus? If superior to neutral, extension is the tone that is called upon for the child. When the focus is toward the floor, there is more of a flexed or stooped posture. For a child most all of the world is above their head. Place neutral eye level targets for them to look at while walking to entrain their balance, coordination and proprioceptors in heel-toe walking. Teach them from their own video as well.

Torticollis. Birth is a tough process. Consider the birth process, history, trauma, induction, C-section and/or if C1, C2, C3 are out of alignment. For torticollis, stretching may not be the only answer. Early treatment of babies zero to six months old via craniosacral gentle manual traction with gentle mobilization (just touching the C2–C3 transverse processes with or without baby moving) has helped to resolve many of these issues. The process is very gentle; as a skilled therapist, you want to think of *lightly touching the transverse processes.*

Therapists also need to consider eye alignment in torticollis cases since the landscape of the child's vision may conform to the misalignment of their head. One of our patients who was referred to us at age four, initially experienced resolution of neck range-of-motion issues after several months of treatment. He was able to walk around with good posture and head and neck alignment. When he ran to kick a soccer ball, however, the head and neck misalignment returned, not because of torticollis but because of visual landscape misalignment. Cases such as this call for a referral to a behavioral optometrist or a pediatric neuro-ophthalmologist for visual rehabilitation; therapists may be able to carry out the visual exercises at home. One of the eyes' most important motions is the ability to cross their own midline.

The therapist brings the child's hands together in front of the patient's eyes then cross hands to one side of the body, then repeat on the opposite side. If a lighted toy and/or noise toy is placed between the child's hands, hearing and vision can be simultaneously stimulated. This technique will also assist in trunk movements in children with a history of stroke. Rotation is a primary movement in eyes, neck, trunk, arms, and legs. Remember PNF (Proprioceptive Neuromuscular Facilitation) patterns? Without rotation, we would move rigidly and have difficulty with balance as well as starting and stopping momentum during gait.

Hold joints rather than muscles to assist in movements. The muscle sensors drive their own movement and can interfere with intended results. For example, in guiding an arm for an activity, hold the elbow and wrist with your index fingers and thumbs. I named "carpals and condyles," this allows the patient to subconsciously concentrate on their own movements. The joints pick up proprioceptive information, and there are fewer skin and muscle belly sensations/contractions delivered at these points of contact.

Helping children cross the center midline is also of keen importance with infants born with agenesis corpus callosum. Their midline actually lies longitudinal along right and left nipple lines. This idea gives new meaning to the midline of the child. Cross-pattern rubbing and brushing of the head, neck, and trunk is from right to left to right.

The brain begins to recognize the "whole" body with this pattern. Follow this by symmetrical stimulation of bilateral upper and lower extremities. Combine physical stimulation with emotional cues. Emotion crosses both hemispheres because it engages the frontal lobe and limbic system without going through the corpus callosum. The limbic system connects to the cortical lobes from the inside. Pairing sensation and emotion will cause signals to travel together across the brain for new connections.

Bring hand to ipsilateral foot, then contralateral foot with increased trunk rotation. Remember that eyes, head, and neck turn first. This also aids as an override to primitive reflex patterns that interfere with active movements of roll, sit, and come to a standing position.

In our clinic, we place a towel sling under the belly to assist in four-point for hands and knees, come to sit, and pull to stand. This technique is helpful if the infant/child avoids prone position due to G-tube or a tracheostomy. It also allows skills to develop and teaches the child how to easily get in and out of positions independently. Move slowly at first, since that is the speed we all learn. As recognition of the skill requirements occur in the child's brain, speed will increase.

Holding a child's hands for ambulation assistance sometimes restricts trunk rotation and balance. Try holding the shirt above the shoulders with assisted rotation of the trunk. This technique with allow easier shift in weight-bearing. Having a patient use a walker also causes decreased trunk rotation and increased difficulty with weight-shifting. Please consider the strap tension on a seat in a gait trainer. Is the seat securing position and/or restricting rotation of the pelvis and trunk? If our goal is to progress the child toward independence in gait, we have to consider assisting the trunk in rotatory components in weight- shifting for balance assurance and function.

Rotation of trunk and extremities are among subconscious motor skills. The Oxford Living Dictionary defines the subconscious as concerning the part of the mind that influences actions without conscious awareness of the individual. The subconscious mind can dictate power over the conscious mind. Through addressing the sensation of rotation components it will bring awareness to the cortical level and the patient will be able to re-pattern movements. The primitive reflexes and —fight, flight, freeze—all influence attention and learning new skills. These qualities reside in lower-brain centers beneath the level of conscious thought. These fast relay systems reside in the area below the cortex and seem to fly past conscious awareness. Environment is an important influence for the child.

Try to make home visits to see what caregivers have to use for working with their child. Also what is the atmosphere in the home? Is it a calm or chaotic environment?

Children are literalists in receptive and expressive language. They operate on "command or requests" and do not necessarily understand the meaning of "no or don't" in a sentence. Hypnosis instructor– Ron Eslinger CRNA reinforced the belief that young children understand positive words and present tense. This is one reason why redirection works well. Young children respond to very short phrases such as "Come," "Sit," "Stay," and "All done." These are also simple in sign language. If "No" is connected with a fearful parent, the child may connect the "No" with fear rather than the meaning of the word.

Related to physical function, what do you not think about that occurs anyway? In the adult, these processes all live in the subconscious mind. Walking, riding a bike, sport or skill becomes automatic with practice. It can be brought back up to the conscious mind if there is a new challenge involved. Walking or riding a bike on a new trail. Learning a golf swing or driving, for example, occurs slowly at first, then speed and accuracy follows. This is a good thought to remember when children are working on new skills.

Evaluate challenges that may stand in the way of functional movements. Some of the challenges are high or low tone, primitive reflexes, and/or responses to balance challenges. All of these functions live in the primitive centers of the central nervous system. They must first be addressed to progress to more complex functional activities and motor skills. If you find for example, that practiced movements of coming to sitting or walking do not seem to progress, consider lower levels of neural connections and resolve precursor skill challenges in working pathways. You will then be able to use patent nervous system connections to build skills.

When you can change the placement of a function in the brain, you can change the level and type of function. One can refine movements as well as change tone and tremor. Changing a placement of a function in the brain occurs when pairing a function that works with one that does not work well (or at all). The brain automatically demonstrates the paired activities in a response during the treatment—for example, vision and hearing following light and sound.

Awareness is the perception of an event, emotion, sensation, and/or object and reaction to that perception. It is a relative concept and may be subconscious or conscious, from an internally or externally generated perception (visceral, thought, or sensory). Basic awareness of internal or external worlds may lie in the brain stem, according to Bjorn Merker, who studied five children missing 80 percent of their brain.

Merker, B. (2007). Consciousness in the Raw..*Science News Online*, September. Sciencenews.org Retrieved July 14, 2015.

Brain Regions

Cerebellum

This part of the brain is in the back of the skull, just under the cerebrum. It is primarily concerned with controlling smooth movement, coordination, and balance. According to Science Alert, Neuroscientists accidently discovered although the cerebellum is around 10% of the brains whole volume, it contains more than 50% of the brain's neurons. Impairments of the cerebellum are related to tremors, flaws in movements producing ataxia, and reward response that can shape behavior.

Little brain

1. Refines motor control and can be effectively rewired through the incorporation of feedback loops.

2. Involved in some cognitive functions such as attention and language

3. Regulates fear, behavior, and pleasure responses

4. Processes and integrates information from sensory systems of spinal cord, and other parts of the brain, and uses the information to refine motor activity

Wolf U, Rapoport MJ, Schweizer TA. 2009. "Evaluating the affective component of the cerebellar cognitive affective syndrome". *J. Neuropsychiatry Clin. Neurosci. 21 (3): 245-53.*

Damage to the cerebellum can result in decreased equilibrium and issues with posture and motor learning. Tremors interfere with the protective response because of the back and forth movements. It is small but contains granule cells (cerebellar neurons) that connect a massive number of connections to the cortex. The cerebellum is responsible for several different types of motor learning, voluntary movements and adjusts to changes in sensorimotor relationships. It is different from other parts of the brain in that most signals move through it from input to output. The cerebellum receives information from the sensory systems traveling up the spinal cord as well as areas of the brain.

Eccles J. Ito M. Szentágothai J. (1967). *The Cerebellum as a Neuronal Machine.* Springer-Verlag P. 311.

Information received from sensation may be environmental, internal processing, interpretation, and feedback loops. The cerebellum is very plastic in nature and renders flexibility for coordination and fine-tuning of movement from input and output information. It also has multiple available tracks for rewiring and neuroplasticity techniques.

Boyden E. Katoh A. Raymond J. (2004). Cerebellum-dependent learning: the role of multiple plasticity mechanisms. *Annu. Rev. Neurosci.* 27: 581-609.

The cerebellum possesses a phenomenal number of connections with the frontal lobe which is responsible for planning, executive decisions, and voluntary motor control. Through research at Stanford University with Mark Wagner, findings reveal additional functions of the cerebellum as relating to reward response and solving tasks which contributes to shaping behavior.

Wagner M, Kim T, et.al. (06 April 2017) Cerebellar granule cells encode the expectation of reward. Nature 544. 96-100.

Corpus Callosum

A canoe-shaped neural fiber bridge called the corpus callosum connects the two hemispheres of the brain. This bridge assists the nervous system in relaying information from one side of the nervous system to the other. In other words, because of the corpus callosum, your right hand will know what your left hand is doing. If there is damage to the corpus callosum or interruption of the important signals through it, the eyes may not work together, and it will be difficult for the hands to come to midline. A baby with damage or interruption through the corpus callosum may have difficulty with successful independent rolling because the right and left eyes, neck, and trunk are not working together as a team.

Corpus Callosum Functions:

1. Left and right cerebral hemisphere communication

2. Integrates sensory, motor, and cognitive functions between the cerebral cortex in one hemisphere to the similar region in the other hemisphere

3. Communicates somatosensory information between the two halves of the parietal lobe and the visual cortex in the occipital lobe

Hofer, S. Frahm, J.(2006). Topography of the human corpus callosum revisited—Comprehensive fiber tractography using diffusion tensor magnetic resonance imaging. *NeuroImage* 32 (3): 989-94.

How should a therapist treat a diagnosis of agenesis of corpus callosum? How can you stimulate crossing to each side of the brain?

Lila

Lila was born without a corpus callosum. She demonstrated low tone, her eyes did not work together, and she did not bring her hands or feet to midline. Midline for an infant with no corpus callosum is lateral to the body midline, closer to the nipple line. Each side of the body may feel like another "whole body." Cross-pattern rubbing and brushing is imperative to send information into the central nervous system for coordination of the halves. Visual tracking left and right provided the first rotary movements crossing midline, this is followed by neck rotation and trunk rotation.

Trunk rotation was difficult for Lila because of the midline misplacement. Lila was given daily exercises of whole-body brushing and brisk hand rubbing with right to left to right patterns. We took care in avoiding the mouth and diaper area. Some philosophies avoid the abdomen area, but in our clinic, we include it. I am a mother several times over, and I washed my babies all over as all mothers and fathers do. We do not prolong treatment over the abdomen, but we want them to recognize they have a "whole" trunk, and this may enable full core stability for motor skill accomplishment. They will use what is within their conscious or subconscious awareness.

After rock, roll, and swing vestibular stimulation followed by visual tracking with rattle and light, Lila's eyes began to work as a team. Depth perception was accomplished, and her hands and feet came to midline.

We have loads of musical instruments in Nashville, and this home was no exception; it had an upright piano. I asked the father if I could hold Lila on the bench for her to play the keys. He said yes. Lila touched individual keys and began to hum. I asked the Father—a singer and songwriter—to please come listen and see if she was humming the note. He exclaimed, "My baby has perfect pitch!" We then found use of music activated additional emotion responses and the limbic system was aided in crossing midline from inside out.

Lila vaulted ahead in progress and was on track for her motor skills. When the hemispheres can work together on sensory information, motor milestones follow. First-things-first. Brain connections are required to progress motor skills as the brain leads the body.

During evaluations, we need to address motor milestone accomplishments and what drives them behind the scenes, which is the nervous system.

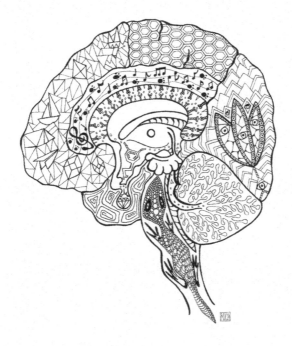

Look closely into the drawing. Reptilian brain – brainstem, Mammal brain – mammary, Limbic system music and emotion and cortex with specific functions.

Limbic System

The limbic system is the emotional brain. It is in contact with all the lobes of the brain. To reach and activate this given function, emotion is added to all treatments. The limbic system also assists in crossing both hemispheres and touching all lobes from the subcortical layers. Techniques for inclusion of emotional components to stimulate the limbic system are an especially important component of treatment strategy. This includes a diagnosis of agenesis corpus callosum, frontal lobe impairment, or any trauma, surgery, or unilateral hemispheric dysfunction.

The limbic system is a complex structure with far-reaching connections. It includes the orbital and medial prefrontal cortex, part of the thalamus, hypothalamus, amygdala, ventral striatum, hippocampus, and cingulate cortex. The hypothalamus, amygdala, and hippocampus are all parts of the limbic system that can be influenced with therapy techniques. Together these areas are involved in motivation (agreement of goals), emotion, learning, and memory. These structures are just beneath the cortex (all are next door to each other in the limbic system).

The emotional portal is in the limbic system. How a patient feels can have a positive or negative effect on learning and milestone attainment. From cheerful praise to abuse or neglect, studies align with results of high or low achievement. In therapy sessions, treatment of the child as well as parent education in home programs supports success. Positive words and praise are an integral part of patients' continued progress in the program. The limbic system receives input from multiple sensory areas and combines them into experiences through association areas.

The limbic system is responsible for:

1. Feeding behavior

2. Aggression

3. Fight and flight behavior

4. Emotional life

5. Formation of memories

6. Increased connections to bilateral hemispheres

7. Responsive to music and can connect hemispheres through emotion in conjunction with the frontal lobe functions.

Thalamus is located along the lateral walls of ventricle number 3. Function can be compromised due to hydrocephalus, central brain structure damage and genetic anomalies to name a few.

1. Processes sensory information (except smell)

2. Relays information to appropriate higher brain centers

3. Sorts and relays incoming sensory information to the appropriate processing area of the cerebral cortex

4. Allows a crude appreciation of pain, temperature, and pressure. Sensation is not localized to a particular area of the body until it reaches the cortex. This allows practitioners to redirect information into different areas of the brain for processing.

5. Neuroplasticity is needed when a part of the brain is damaged. This means particular sensory information in relation to auditory, visual, tactile, gustatory is not able to be processed. Translocation of reception and

interpretation of neural signals to another part of the central nervous system is required.

The hypothalamus is located below the thalamus, above the brainstem, and is part of the limbic system.

Some major functions include:

1. Regulating necessary processes of the body

2. Temperature adjustments

3. Thirst

4. Mood

5. Hunger

6. Behavior – attachment

7. Circadian rhythms

8. Autonomic (subconscious or involuntary) regulation

9. Metabolic processes

10. Growth and development

Hippocampus is located on the floor of the right and left lateral ventricle.

Hippocampus functions:

1. Involved in memory and learning.

2. Relies on sleep for processing memories.

3. Recalls facts and experiences to assist in forming spatial memories

4. What, where and when binds together information from other areas of the brain for processing and integration.

Spreng, R. Mar, R. (2012) I remember you: A role for memory in social cognition and the functional neuroanatomy of their interaction. Brain Research 1428: 43-50.

Simpson, J. A. (Nov 1973) The limbic system. J Neurol Neurosurg Psychiatry 39 (11): 1138-1138.

The hippocampus may be damaged through compressive injuries, hydrocephalus, ventricle abnormalities, shearing injuries, closed head and traumatic head injuries.

Amygdala is located deep in the temporal lobes, anterior to the hippocampus and near the hypothalamus. Additional neighboring structures include the basal ganglia, entorhinal cortex, brain stem, thalamus and is intricately connected with the prefrontal cortex and limbic system. The amygdala detects fear, anxiety, emotion and assists the nervous system to prepare for an emergency.

The amygdala is involved in emotion laden incoming sensory information.

1. Establishes association between various sensory inputs and states of affection

2. Assists in regulating hypothalamic activity by involvement in endocrine and sexual behavior as well as nutrition and hydration.

3. Involved in emotion and decision making

4. Stimulation of the amygdala produces feeling of fear and anxiety

Use of music and lullabies can influence cardiac and respiratory function in premature infants. The neural control of heart rate and breathing is subcortical.

Loewy J, Stewart K, et al. (2013) The Effects of Music Therapy on Vital Signs, Feeding, and Sleep in Premature Infants. *Pediatrics.*

Damage to the amygdala

1. Patients will take bigger risks because of decreased feelings of fear

2. Difficulty understanding beliefs of others

3. Poor interpretation of facial expressions and feelings of others

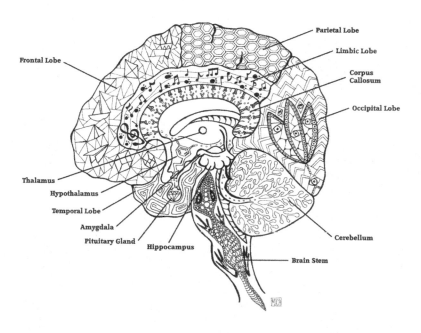

Cerebrum

This is the largest part of the brain and is involved in problem-solving, emotions, and movement. The cerebrum is divided into right and left hemispheres, or halves. In most people, the left half controls movements on the opposite side (the right side), while the right half controls the left side. In most right-hand dominant individuals, the area responsible for language is located on the left hemisphere.

It is important to be aware how important vision is in relation to brain function. Vision is far-reaching and connects to a vast majority of the central nervous system. When a therapist or caregiver intentionally adds vision stimulation to an activity, the brain will connect that activity to other areas of the brain. Vision can connect to the cerebral cortex, vestibular system, hippocampus, basal ganglia, and olfactory bulb (if smell is added).

1. Areas: sensory, motor, meaning

2. Sensory areas – awareness

   a. Skin senses

   b. Vision

   c. Hearing

   d. Olfaction – neurons in the olfactory bulb send axons directly into the olfactory cortex rather than first to the thalamus

3. Motor areas control voluntary movement

4. Association areas are for interpretation and give meaning to

   a. Sensation processing

   b. Speech, language, and communication

c. Thinking, learning memory

d. Decision-making

e. Self-awareness, personality

f. Creativity

Primary somatosensory area provides awareness of general body sensations such as

1. Touch

2. Pressure

3. Vibration

4. Pain

5. Temperature

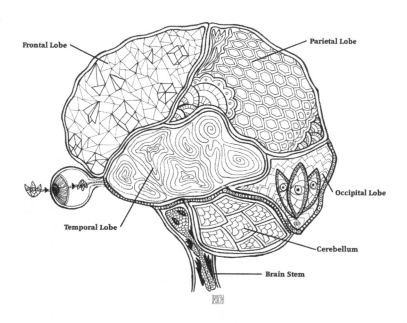

Frontal Lobe

The frontal lobe is large, contains the primary motor cortex, and controls voluntary movements of some body parts. This area also contains most of the dopamine sensitive neurons in the cortex. Dopamine is associated with attention, short-term memory, and motor planning. It assists in the selection of sensory information that arrives in the thalamus and goes to the forebrain. The frontal lobe also is home to executive decision-making. It is the last lobe to mature.

Murphy, E. Benitez-Burraco A.(2016). Gene Slows Frontal Lobes, Boosts Schizophrenia Risk. *National Institute of Mental Health.Frontiers in Human Neuroscience. Retrieved 011219.*

Temporal Lobe

The temporal lobe processes sensory information and files in appropriate categories. This lobe is adjacent to all other lobes in the brain. Visual memories are processed from the hippocampus reception and ingestion. The temporal lobe processes additional information from object to facial perception and recognition. This function is also tied to emotional associations. Primary auditory cortex processes semantics, language comprehension, naming, verbal memory, and wires with vision.

Hickok, G. Poeppel, D.*(May 2007)* The Cortical Organization of Speech Processing. *Nature* (Nature Publishing Group) 8 (5): 393-402.

Parietal Lobe

The parietal lobe demonstrates two functional regions One region is responsible for integration of sensation forming packets of information related to cognition. Information of the second region develops self awareness and body image in the spatial coordinate system for successful movement in the environment. Sensation and perception work primarily with vision to promote integration of information.

The posterior parietal lobe is part of the motor system. This posterior region of the parietal lobe is involved in the pathway for dorsal stream of vision "where" (spatial) and "how" (action). This cortical area combines motor signals as well as controlling hand and eye movement and assists in balance control.

Vision, motor skills and sensory information come together in the parietal lobe for initial motor movements as well as reception of sensory feedback from motor skills. Neuroplasticity is active with sensory stimulation that travels along feedback loops to promote alternate formation of functional pathways.

Parietal Lobe functions:

Mechanoreception – from skin – touch, temperature, pain
Proprioception as it relates to body spatial awareness
Language processing – knowledge of numbers and their relation
Two-point discrimination
Graphesthesia
Touch localization

Goodale, M. Milner A (1992). Separate visual pathways for perception and action. *Trends Neurosci.* 15(1):20-5.

Fogassi L, Luppino G. (2005) Motor functions of the parietal lobe. *Current Opinion in Neurobiology, 15:626-631.*

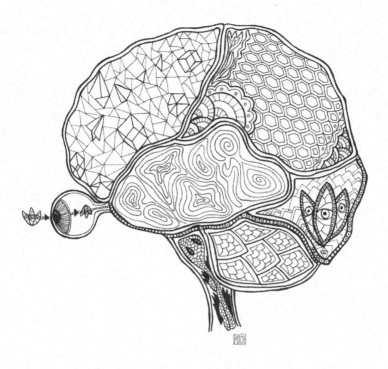

Occipital Lobe functions:

1. There is a difference between sight and vision.

2. Sight – see object as a thing

3. Vision – object has meaning and relevance and usually given a name or sensation

4. The image is inverted on the retina of the eye

5. In the occipital lobe the image and the object is brought upright.

Some visual tasks include visuospatial processing, motor perception, color differentiation, team to promote depth perception and stereoscopic vision. The primary visual cortex is responsible for visual processing information. The occipital lobe receives sensory information from the visual fields and thalamus.

The occipital lobe has pathways or streams for specific information relay systems. The ventral stream is from the primary visual cortex to the inferior temporal cortex. This pathway is associated with "what" object recognition. The dorsal stream is from primary visual cortex to posterior parietal cortex and associated with "where" and "how" motion. If there is damage to one or both of these pathways, the child may have difficulty locating themselves in an environment, memory, playing with toys, and many more challenges.

Saccades are the simultaneous movement of both eyes looking at an object, used to build a three- dimensional map of surroundings. An abnormal movement is nystagmus which is a saccadic-like movement with slow and fast phases. This may be an imbalance of the vestibular system, cerebellum, and/or brain stem. This can be successfully treated with neuroplasticity techniques to combine multisensory vision, hearing, and vibration.

Children with neurological impairments like cerebral palsy, sometimes receive therapy that focuses primarily on their motor skills but overlooks neurological sensory deficits. Patients rely on sensation for initiation of movement, feedback, and motor control. Sensory evaluation and treatment need to be part of assessments and treatments. If treatment does not result in advancing motor skills, change and adjust the sensational cues.

Cooper J. Majnemer A. et al. (1995) The determination of sensory deficits in children with hemiplegic cerebral palsy. *Journal of Child Neurology.*10(4): 300-309.

Children may demonstrate loss of balance and control of gait cycle on even and uneven ground. If bracing is required, on-off use is important to give initial proprioception in heel strike and follow proprioceptive influence in a typical gait cycle. The ankle foot orthosis brace distributes the sensory impact of the foot coming in contact with the floor. The information is delivered in a wider area than the heel and thus disbursement of force into the plantar surface of the foot and to the lower leg. It is optimal therapy to promote full sensory experiences for the children that have central nervous system impairments. In an article by A. H. Hoon et.al. children with cerebral palsy were found to have damage in the posterior thalamic tracks with symptoms of reduced proprioception and motor performance.

Hoon A. Stashinko E. et al. (2009) Sensory and motor deficits in children with cerebral palsy born preterm correlate with diffusion tensor imaging abnormalities in thalamocortical pathways. *Developmental Medicine and Child Neurology.* 51(9): 697-704.

An article by Nashner, Shuway-Cook, and Matin serves to reinforce reasons for neuroplasticity as a treatment program. With regard to maintaining stance, somatosensory, vestibular, and visual stimuli were components of the "sensory organization." The patients' "muscle coordination" was compromised due to the temporal and spatial muscular irregular contractions. The majority of children with cerebral palsy demonstrated atypical muscular coordination unilateral or bilateral, sensory and organization challenges.

Nashner L. Shumway-Cook A. Matin O. (1983) Stance posture control in select groups of children with cerebral palsy: Deficits in sensory organization and muscular coordination. *Experimental Brain Research.* 49(3). 393-409.

A more in-depth understanding of motor control is needed. In our clinic, we have found that a majority of children with damage to the cortex demonstrate primitive reflex patterns. These are active motor movements initiated from below the level of the cortex. We also found that working within range of motion also needs to follow the natural primitive reflex patterning in and out of sequence. To gain additional range of motion in spastic-laden bodies is much easier while the child is asleep since there is little to no spasticity present in a sleeping brain. During sleep, the cortex becomes less active and the midbrain and brainstem are working. If the awake child is in an extension posture in supine, therapists can change the head position to more of a flexed posture. This will release high tone qualities.

During treatments, we integrate simultaneous delivery of a combination of vision, hearing, vestibular stimulation creating a cross-wiring effect. We found it was our job to present stimulation in such a way as to provide multiple synaptic pathway opportunity for development. The central nervous system takes care of the intricate new connections formed.

Patients with cortical vision impairment are capable of developing increased vision in this fashion. Improvements in balance, proprioception, and environmental perception have occurred in our patient population. One of our patients born without eyes demonstrated accelerated balance and negotiation of safe ambulation in his home.

To briefly overview the neural conduction in the peripheral nervous system and the basis of neuroplasticity treatments.

1. The *sensory division* (afferent) – brings sensory information from sensory receptors to the central nervous system.

2. *Motor division* (efferent) – carries motor requests from the central nervous system to the muscles.

3. *Feedback loops* – are involved in autocorrect. These pathways travel into central nervous system areas that process sensory information and then send out alterations to control motor movements.

Autonomic Nervous System

The ANS continuously regulates subconscious control of smooth muscle, glands, cardiac muscle function. Here, there are three divisions: sympathetic, parasympathetic and enteric. The hypothalamus acts as a regulator and integrator for autonomic functions as it receives information from the limbic system.

1. *Sympathetic* division of the Autonomic Nervous System

   • Prepares the body to deal with stressful or emergency conditions (the body's "fight or flight" division)

   • It is difficult to nearly impossible for people to learn and remember while under stress. We must think about caregivers and stress. Some parents are in "fight or flight" for one year after learning about the challenges of their child. The earlier treatment begins, the more quickly positive functional results will occur.

2. *Parasympathetic* division of the Autonomic Nervous System

   • Regulates organ functions for general body maintenance during less stressful times (the "rest-and-digest and feed and breed" division) and learn.

3. **Enteric Nervous System** is the intrinsic neural system of the gastrointestinal system.

   • This system senses chemical and mechanical gut changes

   • Sometimes called the second brain of the body

   • Regulates peristalsis and secretions in the gut

These divisions of the subcortical regions determine a child's ability to accept information, stimulation, and neuroplasticity processes. Think of a baby who is crying or alarmed. In that instance, learning is difficult for them as they may be in fight or flight, hungry, or in pain. Digestion may not be going well, and calming may be needed. Learning and development are important for positive progress to occur.

An article by Alireza Shamsoddini, MOT, compared the effect of NDT treatments versus sensory integration therapy in children with CP, and reported that both sensory integration and neurodevelopmental treatment improved gross motor function. Use of the Gross Motor Function Measure (GMFM) scale revealed improvements in lying to rolling, sitting, crawling, and kneeling and standing. More advanced skills such as walking, running, and jumping did not improve. In the studies, exact techniques descriptions were not presented.

Shamsoddini A. (2010) Comparison between the effect of neurodevelopmental treatment and sensory Integration therapy on gross motor function in children with cerebral palsy. *Iranian Journal of Child Neurology.* 4(1): 31-38.

Russell D. Rosenbaum P. et al. (June 1989) The Gross Motor Function Measure: a means to evaluate the effects of physical therapy. *Developmental Medicine & Child Neurology;* 31: 341-52.

Sensory organ systems

As therapists we want to heighten sensory awareness for use in therapy treatments. Sensation is the entryway into the central nervous system. We actually only have control over sensation. When we work to assist in motor skill correction, the patient picks up sensation of our hands, equipment, movement, and or proprioception changes. Feedback loops offer correction to motor skills demonstrated. If therapy does not change the motor skill, change the sensation delivered.

Naming of the traditional five senses —sight, taste, smell, hearing, touch—has been credited to Aristotle. De Anima. Book II. DA II.7-11 Fortunately science has determined many senses in the human. In therapy sessions, we have a whole host of sensations available for use with neuroplasticity endeavors.

1. Sight – Visual – 80 percent of incoming information, light, color, and motion

2. Smell – Olfactory – very short distance to brain receptors, combines with taste to integrate information into a flavor and memory

3. Taste – regions on tongue map sweet, salty, sour, bitter, and umami (detects amino acid glutamate)

4. Touch – light touch, pressure, vibration, temperature (internal and external), pain, itching

5. Hearing in air or water

6. Proprioception – position of body in space

7. Tension sensors – stretch receptors, monitor muscle tension

8. Nociception – discomfort or pain, cutaneous, visceral, and somatic

9. Equilibrioception – vestibular labyrinthine system, gravity perception in reference to own body, balance with movement and directional changes

10. Stretch receptors – internal organs and vessels, Golgi tendon organ, skin

11. Chemoreceptors – detection of hormones or drugs in blood, medulla region

12. Thirst – hydration levels and urge to drink

13. Hunger – urge to eat

14. Time – sense of time

Neuroplasticity treatments use the sensation. Incoming sensory tracks detour and bypass damaged or missing portions of the brain. Select combinations of stimulation utilize overlapping connections and neural tracks. Hearing, emotion, rhythm, rhyme, and beat all coalesce in music. Music touches on all lobes of the brain and can directly assist in rerouting sensory information into pathways that work. As we study the brain, many of these sensory delivered activities will be apparent as you look from a different viewpoint.

Derek's Story

We were fortunate that Derek was referred to our clinic when he was only six months old. He had already been diagnosed with multiple congenital abnormalities, muscle weakness, blindness, nystagmus, and micro eye size. The earlier treatment could begin, the faster he would demonstrate positive results. In my initial evaluation, Derek demonstrated low tone in his neck, trunk, arms, and legs. His hands were in a semi-fisted position.

Derek also displayed poor head and neck control. He could roll prone to supine but was unable to roll supine to prone position. He did not respond to any visual tracking stimulation. He did respond to auditory tracking, which was a great sign. We searched to find cranial nerves that were functioning since sensory and motor relays in the head and neck are fast and effective pathways for rewiring through feedback loops.

During Derek's second treatment, I gave exercise instructions to his parents and nurse using positioning and sensory education to the head, neck, face, cranial nerves, trunk, arms and legs, and hands and feet. I also gave them instructions on rotational movements to the neck and trunk as well as upper and lower extremities. They received a daily home program to support the neuroplasticity program advancement. Because the brain remembers whatever it does the longest, we instructed mom, dad, and the nurse on treatments, giving them practice and tips for daily use.

Less than three months into Derek's therapy, his case notes noted that he had increased visual tracking to a light in front of him.

His hands were more open and exploring his environment, and he displayed decreased nystagmus.

By the time Derek turned one year old, he had developed good sitting balance and could pull to stand with assistance. At sixteen months, he was able to walk with manual assistance. He was able to walk behind a pushcart independently and negotiate in space without running into furniture. He was also able to reach and grasp a toy in front of him from visual cues alone. At an appointment with his pediatric neuro-ophthalmologist, the physicians said, "I don't know what happened, but your child can see. Thank you for coming today."

Currently, Derek can walk alone without assistance and without verbal cues, and he can negotiate inside his home and school. He can see toys near or far in front of him across the room and catch, throw, and kick a ball.

Movement

The essential first motion to initiate function is rotation. Active movement of the infant/child visually looking side to side is a precursor for rotation of the neck and trunk. These basic rotational movements will later assist in learning, balance in sitting, standing, and ambulation. For example, a child will have much better control of maintaining sitting balance if their head and neck demonstrate independent control of upright posture. Primary use of visual abilities connects to the majority of the brain. Vision also gives feedback to balance systems for control of accurate movements and learning opportunities. If the eyes do not rotate, this may preclude the neck and trunk rotation required for rolling, coming to sit, pull to stand, and walking.

It is imperative for a child to be aware of where their body is in relation to the world and gravity. Sensory stimulation—such as brushing, brisk hand-rubbing of skin of the head, neck, trunk, arms, and legs in a three-dimensional fashion—assists in creating these reference points. Hence, the movements of reach, grasp, crawl, and walk become more attainable.

The infant or child now knows where their three-dimensional body is in relation to the world, allowing more functional coordinated movement to develop. If we ask a person, "Where is the glass of water?" They will say something like, "It is in front of me to the right of my computer." Most people will give directions from their present location.

The semicircular canals are the balance mechanism in the ears. They function within genuine primary engagement and coordinate with body sensations for feedback enabling balance control. This can include head position during movement and gravity changes, proprioception, and vision. Awakening the balance functions allows for an improved speed of development.

Some children may be slow to catch their balance in sitting. This is common in children with low tone. Increased speed of tipping out of upright and/or increasing the angle of departure from midline can spark improved protective responses. Brisk skin stimulation of short duration delivered to the head, neck, trunk, and upper and lower extremities assists in increasing the lower-tone individual to a higher and more typical tone. This therapy technique also allows more competent response to protective responses.

Visual exercises along the X-, Y-, and Z-axis are essential in beginning the striated voluntary muscle control of the eye muscles and coordinated rewiring of the central nervous system. Visual tracking is a tool that can be used for assistance in eye teaming, rotation of head and neck, and decreasing the power of some of the primitive reflexes.

Vision has a vast array of the connections in the brain and is utilized as a pivotal sensation in therapy treatment sessions. According to Conn's Current Therapy, one-fourth of the information relayed to the visual cortex comes through the optic nerves via the lateral geniculate nucleus (part of the thalamus). The other three-fourths come from other cortical centers and may be filtered through attention and other factors.

Bope, E. Kellerman R. (2016) Conn's Current Therapy 2017, *Elsevier Publisher.*

This therapy enrichment opportunity is where neuroplasticity skills may make the most developmental differences. Sensory information in the central nervous system goes into associative areas to be processed and then incorporated for later use. With seven to nine hours of sleep per night, the hippocampus synthesizes information for retrieval in the future. If sleep is interrupted, memory of previous days' skills may not be filed as a functional memory. Neuroplasticity assists in directing specific information to combine for rewiring to occur.

Walker., M (2018) *Why We Sleep: Unlocking the Power of Sleep and Dreams*, Scribner.

Humans have frontal vision, which also infers an organization of the nerve fibers the brain receives from the eyes. The projected image is inverted and flipped left/right and top/down. The lateral geniculate nucleus sends information to the primary visual cortex (striate cortex/Area VI). Because of this connection, each hemisphere is sent information about what is observed by each eye.

When eyes look in the same direction, stereoscopic information occurs and is processed as depth perception becomes available. Visual signals are processed at multiple regions in the visual system. This system between the eyes and the brain allows for feed-forward and feed-back loops between levels. These functions are essential for motor planning and correction of movements to maintain balance and accuracy. Let us also think of the neuroplasticity qualities of vision. Directional eye movement gives power to or removes the influence of a primitive reflex. This action also feeds-inferior into the brainstem and feeds-superior to the cortex in the central nervous system.

Nearly every part of the brain has a connection to vision. The occipital lobe is the major entry point specifically for visual information. The parietal lobe associative region in the right hemisphere is dedicated to the manipulation of objects, reach/grasp, touch, and sight. The parietal lobe associative region in the left hemisphere is employed in words or ideas that are read or spoken as well as in long-term reflexive memory.

The temporal lobe is involved in long-term declarative or pictorial memory with the right hemisphere, whereas the left hemisphere is involved with verbal memory. The frontal lobe is concerned with storing the location of objects that were seen, maintaining object permanence, and planning sequential movements. The occipital lobe sends two pathways through MT and V4. Multiple connections assist vision with integration between these pathways. The MT toward the parietal cortical area creates the "where" pathway. This pathway functions with relation to location plus motion or anticipated movements. The V4 tracks progress toward the inferotemporal cortex to make the "what" pathway. This route works in conjunction with forms, colors, object recognition, and memory.

Neuroplasticity is greatest in early childhood, as stated in a December 2016 article by Tailor, V. Schwarzkoph, D and Dahlmann-Noor. Case studies show that before age two, neural development is rapid. Change in sensory perception shows that alterations and adaptions quickly occur. Between the ages of six and eight, the critical period of vision development is closing and the treatments for vision correction will happen more slowly.

Tailor, V. Schwarzkoph, D. Dahlmann-Noor., A. (2017) Neuroplasticity and amblyopia: Vision at the balance point. *Curr Opin Neurol.* Feb;30(1):74-83.

In our practice, we try to attend to vision exercises before the patient reaches one and a half years old. After age two, without remediation of torticollis, a child's landscape may remain tilted. That child can walk with his or her head and neck erect, but running or navigating uneven ground may result in a head tilt to reframe the landscape so that it appears level in the brain in order to maintain balance. Torticollis drastically changes the orientation of the eyes and ears in contrast to the landscape in the world and on the page that a child wants to read. Effective and early treatment will bypass frozen, tilted landscapes. It will also enhance visual competency and proficiency needed for running, writing, and reading.

A majority of primitive reflexes originate from deep within the lower neurological centers in the brainstem and are important to early movements. These are subconscious reactions and movements. Integration of primitive reflexes is important to ensure that voluntary movements are freely allowable. Use of primary senses, such as vision, and movements with connections adjacent to the seat of the primitive reflexes serve to decrease the power of the reflexes and influence integration more rapidly.

Rotational motions of the eyes, neck, upper and lower extremity, and trunk are required for successful rolling, come to sitting, balance in sitting, and walking. While therapists work on developmental skills, rotational components are imperative for success. Rotation of the upper extremity can empower the child to utilize their voluntary components of motion for action desired, such as balance, holding an open hand for reaching and grasping.

Hold the wrist and elbow joints, then proceed with active assistive range of motion, slowly move in internal and external rotation of the arm. Avoid holding to the muscle belly or tendons so the tone of the flexors is not increased. Rolling in as much extension of the upper extremity as possible reduces the torque force on the shoulder, elbow, wrist, and hand. (Roll like a clay snake.) This technique assists the child in decreasing the involuntary force of palmar grasp reflex evidenced by the flexed side of Asymmetrical Tonic Neck Reflex. Proper hand placement by the therapist is essential in guiding movements of the arms and legs.

When a child experiences a stroke or part of the higher-brain centers demonstrates impaired function, the child's brain will relinquish control to the lower central nervous centers, which then take on a more powerful role. In a child or an adult who has had a stroke on the left side of the brain, like the middle cerebral artery, the right arm and hand may be flexed and held tightly against the chest with hand closed with the lower extremity in extension. This spastic force looks and acts like the Asymmetrical Tonic Neck Reflex.

When higher-brain center's integration and overriding mechanisms are compromised, influences of the lower centers become evident. Skilled and directed integration techniques are useful in these instances. Remember that the brain builds from the brain stem to the cortex and lobes from back to front, while the body develops from the top down. Therapy exercises and stimulation should be delivered in that order so that the brain can receive stimuli in an orderly fashion and integrate the information more readily.

How We Learn

Children learn with intention and are trained via repeated tasks. It will only take a few minutes daily to incorporate activities and exercises into the child's life. (eliminate for example, performing a stimulating massage at bath time.) Rock, roll, and swing for play.

Frequency, pairing at least two senses, and novelty are key to neuroplasticity.

Think about a man driving a car. He was once a beginner who had to consciously concentrate to learn where the keys and steering wheel were (hand memory and movements), understand his position in relation to the road and the car (vision and reading), accurately place his feet on the pedals, and maintain control of his head, neck, and trunk just to name a few tasks. After repeated practice, these movements "floated down" in his nervous system and became more subconscious and automatic.

Just like a young adult learning to drive a car, a child will learn from repetition of activities, which will become automatic and easier. Tone changes, moving away from obligatory primitive reflex patterns, and increasing active voluntary motions will free the child to catch up to their developmental milestones.

It is important to keep in mind how the various areas of the brain are connected to each other. The brain can receive information, integrate the stimuli, make sense of the world, and respond appropriately. Pathways in the nervous system are laid down at an incredible rate. The more information a baby is exposed to, the more quickly the basic nervous system functions will build skills and reinforce integration. When the foundation of learning is strengthened, additional highly functioning pathways can be added, preserved, developed, and formed successfully. In other words, more diverse information equals more learning and the development of new abilities.

Without stimulation, exposure, and encouragement, unused pathways are abandoned and become nonfunctional. Treatment including rolling and crawling serves to strengthen ambulation abilities. The central nervous system conserves its energy expenditure to furnish nourishment of oxygen, glucose, and synaptic stimulation to the pathways that are used frequently. Progress can regress unless new, novel, and interesting activities are introduced to the baby.

Covering body parts in need of stimulation, balance feedback and integration, as in the use of AFOs, DAFOs, etcetera, let us use caution. If body parts are constantly covered, the brain will forget use and prune un-needed connections. Supports made with foam can be compressed with 15 pounds of pressure. Most all children using these are over 15 pounds. Consider gel supports for calcaneal and arch alignment. If children need supports please instruct parents on-off wearing, or the neural connections may be cut off. Also, check the anterior tibialis and gastroc soleus strength before application of a brace and after 6 months. In our clinic, we found, patients that transferred to our care that had constant daytime brace wear demonstrated bilateral foot slap, foot drop and increased ligamentous instability of ankles in weight bearing.

Avoid repeating the same activities the same way. In the book *Movements that Heal* by Harald Blomberg, MD, and Moira Dempsey, development and rhythmic therapy of the child is discussed. Movement patterns in the body after birth begin as breathing. This movement is central, essential, and at the core of the baby's development. Mouthing is also one of the most sensitive parts of the body and used for feeding, exploring, reaching, grasping, and letting go. The body has connectivity from several different directions: core/distal, head/tail, upper/lower, body/half and cross/

lateral connectivity. These can all be used for sensory stimulation directional therapy.

- **Core/distal** connects the umbilicus to the extremities. This helps the baby realize where they are and that the rest of the world surrounds them.
- **Head/tail** This describes top-down organization of sensory information and development.
- **Upper/lower** connects the top/bottom halves of the body and enables stability.
- **Body/half** assists with differentiation of right and left sides of the body and allows movement in all directions.
- **Cross/lateral** connects coordination of the opposite arm and leg to move in patterns.

Blomberg, H., & Dempsey, M. (2011) *Movements that heal: Rhythmic movement training and primitive reflex integration*. Sunnybank Hills, Qld.: Book Pal.

Let's back away from the anatomy of the brain and divide it into additional areas so we can enter diverse sensory information. We want to look at the two minds to consider – conscious and subconscious.

Conscious mind functions:

1. Language

2. Question and response

3. Action and interaction

4. Learning new tasks – practice delivers a task into the subconscious mind (Ex: learning to serve a tennis ball, practice, get the ball to desired location, miss the target – may not know what went wrong because action came

from the subconscious rather than conscious mind, watch your video)

5. Retraining gait – make a video of the patient, and have the patient/parent watch it, because without seeing the video, the patient's motions are in the automatic/subconscious mode and difficult to retrieve back to the conscious mind.

The subconscious mind is in the present tense. Functions happen in the background beyond cortical and conscious awareness.

1. Intention

2. Tone of voice

3. Touch

4. Stimulation

5. Movement

6. Interaction

7. Attention to task and surroundings

8. Filters and filtering background

9. Sleep and in-between

10. Memory setting in, when to use learned task, when to design new response

11. Primitive reflexes

12. Balance and responses – sitting and standing balance

13. Repeated and practiced tasks – tie shoes, dress self, drive, lock door

14. Walking – remember learning? Remember heel-to-toe instead of toe walking?

How can we devise a method to encompass the functions for a format for treatment? Design information to enter and be accepted and go beyond the conscious and subconscious filters. Sensory information will be sent to specific regions and association areas for processing and possible integration. Addition of balance challenges may bring ambulation into a more conscious realm for techniques to be refined.

Brandon's Story

A golden child with blond hair and blue eyes, Brandon was the love of his mother's life. But by the time he turned two years old, she knew something was wrong. Where he had once been playfully interactive with others, now he was withdrawn. Where he had been developing along normal and predictable lines, now his vocabulary was lagging. He refused to make eye contact, reach out toward others, or laugh, and eventually he stopped initiating conversation and interacting.

It would be another two years before Brandon's family would bring him to our clinic. During those two years, his mother and father would take him to numerous specialists to see if anything could be done to awaken their oldest son. Tearfully, Brandon's mother recalled, "My husband and I started our battle by enrolling Brandon in a state university pediatric program until he turned four and we transitioned him to a children's hospital. As we worked with various professionals, locally and regionally, it became apparent that the best results were coming from the professionals who possessed a positive and optimistic attitude, where, above all, they challenged Brandon and didn't give up."

But in the end, nothing seemed to be working. It was time for an outside-the-box approach. This is when Brandon's family made an appointment at our clinic to Discuss the neuroplasticity program.

"We read on the internet about Dr. Pryor," said Brandon's father, "and saw the videos where she'd done all of this work with children with spina bifida, Down Syndrome, and autism, so it seemed that maybe she would be the next logical step for us."

As they walked into the clinic, I spoke to them about the program, but mostly I spent time with Brandon, never stressing him out or pushing him to do anything he didn't want to do. I told his mother that every child is unique, and it was our mission to find his *unique genius.*

Also, I informed his parents that from my initial time spent in the exam room with them, Brandon seemed to be very intelligent and showed potential signs of waking up to life outside of his own parameters. I reassured Brandon's parents that their son was able to learn. He was most likely very cognizant and ready and able to learn, but his ability to reach out to others was not connected neurologically. I assured Brandon's mother that she had come to the right place for therapy; our clinic specializes in neuroplasticity and rewiring the brain circuits.

Over the next year or so, I learned that Brandon was very particular with the foods he would eat, although he rarely refused the candy that was offered as reward for cooperative behavior in school. It also became extremely clear that he was very intelligent. He would recite *Superman* and *Thomas the Train* movies. He often used different voices for the different characters, as well as talking to the unseen. His mind seemed to flow on several tracks simultaneously.

One day, my twenty-five-year-old son, Jett, and I worked together with Brandon in the gym section of the clinic. My son tends to be very intuitive when working with children. After a short amount of time, Jett said that Brandon seemed unable to interpret his surroundings and felt fearful about what may be safe and uncertain about what was real and what was not. Brandon also demonstrated echolalia, which is the tendency to repeat things that a person has heard. Jett felt this repeated behavior appeared frequently because Brandon heard the words and he may have felt safe in repeating them. Let us remember, every child is different.

We both agreed that Brandon might be one individual who had the ability to see and hear at a wider frequency spectrum than most. As we age, the spectrum we hear and see becomes more narrow. That would explain why people continually asked Brandon, "What are you doing?" or, "Why are you talking to empty space?" as is the case with many children. In reality, what if we, as adults, are the limited beings? Brandon was drawn to, and was able to receive, accurate information from a computer screen or a television. We wondered if we could design a type of clothing that was illuminated like a television or computer screen. If the teacher wore the illuminated clothing, maybe Brandon would be more encourage to pay attention in class.

Jett and I, being of like mind and thinking on many tracks , decided to incorporate several simultaneous activities with Brandon. Jett was the engineer of activities on one particularly amazing day. That day, a *Thomas the Train* video was playing on the television. For the kinesthetic hunger, since Brandon was quite athletic, we placed him on a stationary bike and requested that he pedal the bike while blowing bubbles.

The combination of activities seemed to open a veil for Brandon and allowed his mind to find purchase. He was conversant and logical and said, "I'm tired of riding this bike and want to get off of it." Then he looked at us directly and smiled. We wondered if this practice could be applied to others with autism. Convinced this was a breakthrough for Brandon, we decided to share the experience we had with his mother and the teachers in his school.

We talked to his mother and explained the activities we wanted her to incorporate in Brandon's daily life. We guided her to ask Brandon questions about what he sees or hears and to remain open and nonjudgmental. She agreed to our plan, feeling that Brandon would continue to cognitively step into our world. We all believed he would be able to progressively learn, talk, relay his needs and express emotion. Even though we asked permission to work with Brandon in seemingly unconventional ways, his mother had confidence in our years of experience with pediatrics and trusted us.

We customized an individual program for Brandon that contained elements of sensory stimulation combined simultaneously with visual and kinesthetic activities. Brandon reacted with increased attention and seemed bored or uninterested when treated otherwise.

The next school year was challenging for six year old Brandon. I asked Brandon's teacher to reward him in ways other than giving him candy. Also, his mother restricted the sweets at home. I suggested the integrated multisensory therapy approach to Brandon's teachers, and Brandon's parents continues to use these techniques. It is imperative that teachers in classrooms have the time and resources to interact with all of the delayed children during the activity time. Simple method of adding a sensation by placing a puzzle or pencil in a refrigerator before use.

I saw Brandon two times a week during that school year. We worked together on the multisensory dimensional therapy program we called "Parallel Play." A great deal of time, respect, listening, and support was going toward Brandon's attempts to relay information and communicate with his family and with me. He was learning additional communication skills and showing good progress. Jett and I had great hopes that Brandon would soon be in "our world."

One thursday morning, Brandon's mother caught my arm and said with tears brimming in her eyes, "You were right! You were right about Brandon. He's awake and with us!" Remarkably, that morning in his usual therapy session, he'd reached out, made eye contact, and connected for the first time in many years with his mother, who had never given up on him. Her voice broken with emotion, she said, "He's going to be able to learn and be like other kids. Thank you! Thank you! It's taken all these years, and you didn't give up."

It is moments like these that make the unconventional nature of my program worthwhile. I thanked her for being so willing to try some of my seemingly far-fetched therapies, and then we both hugged each other. Brandon's nervous system was awake, conversant, and able to learn in the classroom. For the first time in years, he had turned to look at his mother and smiled.

Brandon continued to blossom and grow. His mother routinely called in to report that Brandon looked forward to going to school and the social opportunities to interact with other children had made a world of difference in her son. The frequent smiles that came across his face when I popped my head in the door of his homeroom warmed my heart and made me so very grateful. Brandon was also proud!

I learned so much from Brandon and his parents. In particular, I realized the need for practitioners to understand that each child is as individual with distinct learning potential and function. Partnering with all the people in Brandon's life—from the school system to his parents, grandparent, brother, his family's friends, and all of those involved in his life—was just as integral as the therapies we administered at the clinic. We taught home exercises, skill attainment, and goals to everyone so they were all on the same page. Everyone contributed to therapeutic exercises and integrated them into everyday play.

Questions for the therapist during an evaluation:

- Is the patient relaxing or reacting?

- What part of the nervous system is active?

- What portions of the central nervous system are inactive?

- Remember, it is difficult to learn in fight-or-flight mode.

Look, Listen, and Feel the environment.

- *Look* to see if the environment is conducive to learning.

- *Listen* to what is said and not said; is the patient hungry?

- *Feel* for if the home is safe and the patient is able to play outside.

How do we get into a patient's subcortical functions? With subcortical function relay systems intact, the more complex skills are able to build on top. Midbrain and brainstem functions, primitive reflex elicitation, cranial nerve stimulation influence higher cortical connections, as in creeping and crawling.

Tone thoughts

- Does neuroplasticity make a difference in the tone qualities of the baby?

- How can we change tone?

- Sensory stimulation can inhibit or assist in integration of primitive reflexes, progress responses, and change in muscle tone.

Reticular Activating System

The reticular activating system connects the brain stem to the cortex. It is important in the asleep-to-awake state and times of high attention. It receives signals from visual, vestibular, auditory, proprioceptive, and tactile senses and sends them to the cortex for processing. Tone can be re-regulated through this system.

Changing Tone

High tone – Overstimulation of body parts that demonstrate high tone to numb and dumb the reactivity of spasticity. High tone is sensory driven and continued brushing, vibration will decrease tone. Therapists will be able to feel the tone change.

Low tone – To increase tone, use quick stimulation of a vibrator, a brush, or brisk hand-rubbing, cool pack, quick rock, roll, and swing with short duration. The therapist wants to wake up the nervous system.

The therapist narrates the exercises and sensory activities during the treatment session. Treatments of the patient go into the sensory system and language reception of the child. Teaching and explanation to the parents may go through the sensory system and prefrontal cortex. It is to the child's advantage to have the parents observe the treatment, practice the skills, and gain feedback from the practitioner. Ask parents or caregivers to attend therapy sessions so they can do the exercises daily; if not, the child will progress very slowly or not at all.

PT Phone Home Program: The Use of Video in Therapy

I recommend capturing video recordings of your child for reference in therapy. Look back at your videos each week or month and notice the differences. Show these videos to your medical doctor and your therapists. Since most children will not reliably perform on cue, a recording of your child showing the areas of concern or motor developments that are exciting will allow your medical practitioners to readily *see* your questions.

Some children you encounter in your practice may have specific diagnoses of learning or developmental delay, while other children remain undiagnosed, frequently due to the difficulty of evaluating and testing these children. It may take several sessions to fully understand what is happening with their movements, reactions, and reflexes. In these cases, videos from caregivers are often very helpful in diagnosis. These videos may allow you to observe the child's reactions and movements in their home environment to gain a better understanding of their condition. Videos, both from home and from the clinic, may be sent to a child's physician to assist with coordination of care.

Video capturing an unusual demonstration of movement, tremors, nystagmus in a particular position, or an example of delayed integration of a primitive reflex will allow a child's pediatrician or other treatment providers to observe movements, reactions, and reflexes that are not easily apparent on-the-spot. Videos showing movement of lower extremities in children with spina bifida are frequently helpful when requesting lower extremity bracing supports or a walker. Before sharing any photos or videos with any medical professional for the purposes of diagnosis or teaching, however, you must obtain a signed release from the child's parent or guardian.

Photos and videos can be placed in the electronic medical records. A full and thorough evaluation and treatment plan, updated often, will not only enable a child's development but will also enhance the lives of the child's family as well.

Video and photo the child before and after treatment with the caregiver's phone/camera using both typical speed and slow motion. Remember that you cannot go back in time; your brain will edit the memory of previous signs and symptoms. Have caregivers keep the videos on their phones for follow-up and progress comparison. In addition, have the family sign a photo/video release for you to record them on your own equipment.

Memory of Home Program

Use of the home program results in patients' and family enhanced memory and compliance with video recording on the parent's phone. Many times, home programs that give instructions via paper in English are not always as helpful as we would like them to be. With PT Phone Home Program, caregivers are able to follow the photos and videos on their phone, especially if they are performing teach-back with their child.

Prefrontal cortex processing for parents

Give caregivers home programs that are easy to follow and integrate into their busy day. Consider the following items, which influence parents' understanding and home exercise compliance. Remember to consider fight or flight and stress which can make the cortical memory abilities shut down.

1. Abstract thinking

2. Long-term planning

3. Logic

4. Rationality

5. Judgment

6. Cause-effect

7. Reasoning

8. Motivation

9. Individuality

10. Personality

Teach the Caregiver

What makes sense to the caregiver? Try to make it relatable. Base information on tasks they are familiar with already. Replicate treatment for the child on the parent with sensory stimulation, swing and eye tracking. Include as many senses as possible during each exercise. Remember that whatever fires together will wire together, and neuroplasticity techniques deliver important ways for the nervous system to rewire itself.

Simple activities to add to treatment sessions:

Music - Children store long-term memories of relative pitches, duration of tempo, and timbre-specific information of songs from their infancy.

- Singing – therapist or child

- Rhythm – with consideration of momentum

- Smell – scent the room with calming essential oils on a cotton ball in the corner of the room (avoid eucalyptus and peppermint due to possible sinus irritation)

- Modulation motion of muscular movements

- Activities – come to sit, crawl/creeping pattern, pull to stand, walking

Practices should move from conscious thinking to subconscious activity through practice; for example, walking, fly-fishing, serving a tennis ball, dancing, driving.

How do you remember...?

1. Book – Try to quote "Goldilocks and the Three Bears"

2. Music, rhyme and kinesthetic movements – Itsy Bitsy Spider

3. Sing "Happy Birthday" - Rhyme, emotion, and music like "Happy Birthday" will bring back memories faster because of the limbic components.

Trainor L, Wu L, Tsang C. (2004) Long-term memory for music: infants remember tempo and timbre. *Developmental Science.* 7(3): 289-296.

Music helps reduce heel-stick pain reactions and stress in premature infants. How can this help with calming the nervous system? Are there environmental threats, chaos? Is there difficulty with sensory processing? Evaluate if the child is in fight or flight or has suffered previous trauma. Consider using the "Adverse Childhood Experiences Score."

Tramo, M. Lense, M. et al. (2011) Effects of music on physiological and behavioral indices of acute pain and stress in premature infants: clinical trial and literature review. *Music and Medicine. 3(2): 72-83.*

To assure rapid progress, daily home program compliance is necessary. Caregivers singing and talking through treatments while narrating activities sustains infant attention. Rhyming or singing lyrics with exercises also helps with sequence and memory of exercises for the child and parent.

Nakata, T. Trehub, S.(2004) Infants' responsiveness to maternal speech and singing. *Infant Behavior and Development.* 27: 455-456.

Since a baby has cephal-caudal sequence developmental pattern, new neurological files introduced to the brain will accept information in that same sequence. To follow this pattern, begin by delivering sensory stimulation at the head, then move to the neck and trunk, followed by the arms and legs. This helps the brain form networks to work together for developmental motor skills. As the primitive reflexes become more and more integrated into the background, the higher development functions are refined and accomplished.

Additional sensory stimulation in combination will assist the one hundred billion neurons the infant is born with to branch and form connections and synapses. At birth, each neuron may have 2,500 connections. This number may rise to 15,000 by the time the child is three years old. These neural connections require novel and repeated novel use or they will be pruned.

Shonkoff,, J. & Phillips, D. (2000) *From Neurons to Neighborhoods: The Science of Early Childhood Development* National Academies' Press.

Ten-Year Clinical Study

A ten-year study in our clinic with non-challenged and challenged toddlers between the ages of birth and three years old yielded surprising data. At the outset of the study, the toddlers in the non-challenged group displayed typical physical and neurological growth and development in relation to their peers, whereas the challenged toddlers were experiencing some physical and neurological developmental delays. In this study, parents, caregivers, and childcare providers were instructed in the neuroplasticity program specific to their child. For a few minutes every day, novel exercises were integrated into the toddlers' normal activities. The results were profound.

After the formal therapy program, the children were followed into the classroom setting. Non-challenged children were offered advanced placement while the challenged children were placed in classes with their age-group typical peers. The parents and caregivers noted that both groups of children were friendly and social with classmates.

Two children with Down syndrome were placed in a non-challenged classroom. All children from both groups were coordinated in fine and gross motor skills. Both the non-challenged and challenged children walked before or shortly after their first birthday, and language soon followed. Their visual motor skills, which are essential for reading and comprehension, were also highly developed.

Introduction of novel and challenging therapy practices to the children in both the challenged and non-challenged groups in this study resulted in accelerated development of all the children's fine and gross motor skills as well as their verbal skills. The children were not pushed to improve; they were simply given opportunities for directed play to connect multiple parts of their brain. The children who did not participate in the advanced study program displayed typical skill development.

The entire program utilized natural techniques to enhance education, physical development, awareness, and processing in the newborn all the way up to 11 years of age. The children participating in the study were able to catch up and sometimes surpass their non-involved peers. Parents were allowed to continue the program as long as they liked.

In our clinic, some of the parents noted that their children advanced so much they thought they were finished with therapy. Parents who continued with the advanced programs clearly saw the connection of their children through enhanced neural connections, development, improved function, and reasoning. There were no known complaints about the program or the testing. The activities were integrated into the normal daily routine to prevent extra work or time and provided a therapeutic way to play and handle the child.

As a therapist I highly recommend advanced technological use with home exercise techniques. In our clinic we treat children from multiple countries. The recording of the activities seems to go beyond language. See it – do it. The PT Phone Home Program information is introduced to the baby's nervous system through a variety of pathways. The interaction and responses of the child can be observed during or after the parent, caregivers, and therapists guide activities and "play exercises."

Early Intervention and Developmental Progress

Parents, caregivers, teachers, childcare providers, early intervention programs, and therapists are able to provide daily practice and care to babies and children. The more practice these individuals have with their little ones, the more improvement they will witness. What if the baby was beginning to crawl but was only able to practice crawling one day a week for one hour? This may sound absurd, but it happens. This book and the course of study were written to help bring more understanding of development and home exercises to the parents. When practitioners gain permission to video the child during the evaluation process, follow-up videos will encourage caregivers as they see the progress of their child.

The sooner a child can see a therapist the better. As soon as the caregiver suspects a need , the therapist should ask for an order for an evaluation from the child's physician. A thorough evaluation will render scores from testing and possible neurological deficiencies, then plans for the appropriate therapy program can follow. Many children fall through the cracks when a "wait and see" attitude is adopted. When we "wait and see," time is lost in the neuroplasticity of the brain, and the child will fall farther behind and possibly develop substitution patterns.

The brain has windows of time in which vision and focus develop and the child acquires skills and development milestones like walking and talking. Major milestones are expected at least every three months. If these developments are delayed, the amount of work for the caregivers and child are increased and therapy prolonged. The opportunistic windows of development are open in proximity to the timeline of the milestone attainment marks. For example, if a child does not walk between twelve to sixteen months of age, it may be more difficult for them to develop walking later. If a child is five years old and working to establish an independent gait, the amount of activity and work at home and the clinic to accomplish this will be significant. That said, let me add...it can be done. Directed play activities can help the progression of the child's mind connections and their physical development.

As therapists, we know that most of our patients have neurological changes, omissions, or damage that must be considered when planning their rehabilitation programs. Their bodies are perfect; it is the nervous system that dictates misconnected information, which is then demonstrated in the body. High and low tones are just two of the neurologically influenced impairments we treat. "Management" of atypical tone means it is still there. Through neuroplasticity techniques, we are able to progress toward typical tone, functional and voluntary motions.

In the literature to date, neuroplasticity is a hot topic, but surprisingly little research has been done on how neurological connections relate to motor skill attainment and how to change the connections for greater function. The research that *is* available shows that early intervention screening not only saves money but also increases the efficiency of therapy. However, few detailed techniques are available for application. It is my hope to make skills available to the therapy community.

Studies specifically show that early intervention of therapy can accelerate skill advancement. The younger the patient when therapy begins, the more pronounced these advancements can be. A study by Duke University found that children enrolled in North Carolina's early childhood initiative programs Smart Start or More at Four demonstrated a drastically reduced likelihood of being placed into special education programs by the time the students had reached the third grade.

http://www.smartstart.org/duke-research-shows-smart-start-increases-third-grade-test-scores-reduces-need-for-special-education/ retrieved 011719.

The reduced need for special education classes for these children not only saved a significant amount of money for the state of North Carolina in education costs but also demonstrated the importance and effectiveness of early intervention therapy. When the cause of a developmental challenge is directly treated with neuroplasticity techniques, the progress is faster and self-reinforcing. Advanced training in neuroplasticity will universally produce skilled therapists who can attend directly to the nervous system to connect and advance children's motor skills.

The cost and timesaving effects of early intervention can be seen not only on a state level but also on an individual level. The earlier therapy begins, the more effective it is, saving time and money while also allowing the child's development to more closely match that of his or her peers.

It is important for therapists and educational professionals who are active in early intervention programs to understand that the nervous system is the basis for function. The networks of neurological influence must be considered when trying to establish development of higher skills. For example, it is difficult to teach a child to read when they cannot visually track. If a child has spasticity on one side of their body, they will have difficulty rolling both ways and coming to a sitting position. Both of these skills are dictated by neural connections.

Though a child may be in therapy one to two hours per week, therapy cannot end there. The brain learns whatever it does the most. Think about learning to play the piano. Practice must be daily to be proficient. Playing the piano involves 2 eyes, 2 ears, posture in sitting, 2 hands and processing 2 lines of music as well as feet on the pedals. Function and mobility also involves 2 eyes, 2 ears, posture and so on.

Follow-up and active parenting therapy skills are imperative in the home. . Many parents have toys with light and rattle to play with, but need to be instructed on how to use them for therapeutic intervention. Teach several simple activities and exercises to caregivers so therapeutic play can be performed daily in the home setting. Example: When it is time to eat, work on visual and auditory tracking. Bath time is an opportunity for brushing the body and extremities.

In our clinic, we utilize expanding skills to extend therapy services and empower the caregivers. Therapy exercises and interventions through neuroplasticity techniques were performed daily at home with caregivers. We found great advancements were observed with children having multiple disabilities entering the school system into regular classrooms.

If you believe a program is not working, change it. If you believe the program is working, don't change it. Watch for pitfalls, holes, time wasted, dark places, and nonproductive locations, and ultimately go with what works. Remember you never step in the same nervous system twice. Do a quick re-evaluation of the child each time you see them. They have had experiences since you saw them last that may have influenced skill attainment.

Integration or coordination of the senses and reflexes is fundamental to therapy that makes strides forward. Once a level of therapy is found that works and is integrated, you can work to advance the child's skills. Building blocks in the nervous system connections require linking and rerouting before the next motor skill may be attained. Look for obligatory responses, tone changes with positions, eye alignment, or delays. Each child is different, but challenges can be avoided or reduced when caught early.

Evaluation of
Developmental Milestones

How do you know if a child is developing and progressing? While each child is unique and will develop at their own pace, there are specific developmental milestones that are typically reached by certain ages to demonstrate typical brain growth, neurological and functional development. Numerous formal rating tests exist to identify delays in childhood physical, social, emotional, and neurological development.

All of these tests are utilized as evaluation tools and scored. Repeated evaluations are used to reveal if therapy is successful or if treatment methods need to be changed. If testing reveals that your child is not advancing, change what you are doing. Step backwards in the development timeline of their physiological connections. See what the neurological precursor is for the milestone that they are struggling to achieve. Address that layer of central nervous system first before moving forward. This will allow functional and integrated movement patterns. If not addressed, a splint will not rewire or teach the nervous system. To develop function and neurological connections in an effort to produce improved motor patterns, we will only use on-off splinting as a last resort because the theft of sensory components required for learning.

Most of the infant/child's body is perfect, yet the brain challenges have altered the demonstration of milestone attainment. When there is spasticity present or low tone, we are seeing the symptoms of neurological changes. MRI, FMRI, CT scans and EEGs can basically reveal function of the central nervous system. These tests do not give us results on the neuron, dendrite or axon status. Fortunately, delivering targeted rewiring activities, the stimulus and synapses firing assist in developing additional pathways and connections. As therapists, you are able to do specific testing to determine the most primitive functioning pathways and begin therapy there.

When a child is demonstrating primitive motor functions, the central nervous system is also functioning at that level. In motor milestone language, they may be in the reptilian brain level where rotational abilities are not present, if they cannot turn over. When a patient cannot balance or come to sitting, they may be functioning in the mammal brain arena of connections. This not only tells us how to treat but also how to talk to the patient. Reaching deep into a neurological evaluation may reveal where to start therapeutic interventions.

The Center for Disease Control's website has a detailed list of milestones that can be used by parents to ask for help from medical professionals.

https://www.cdc.gov/ncbddd/actearly/milestones/index.html retrieved 011919

By the age of two months, your child typically will be able to

- Turn their eyes and head toward people and sounds

- Bring their hands to their mouth

- Coo

- Be able to hold their head up while lying prone

By the age of four months, your child typically will be able to

- Copy movements and facial expressions

- Be able to prop themselves up in prone position

- Roll over both ways

- Be able to support their body weight on their lower extremities

- Babble

- Respond to cuddling and play

- Reach for a toy

- Be able to use visual and auditory skills to track objects

- Demonstrate head and neck control

By the age of six months, your child typically will be able to

- Watch themselves in a mirror

- Begin making vowel and consonant sounds

- Have use of bilateral hands for activities

- Come to sitting and sit without support

- Display four-point static and dynamic rocking in position

- Demonstrate trunk control

By the age of nine months, your child typically will be able to

- Use their finger to point to learn about his environment

- Display object permanence

- Copy body movements and play games

- Pull themselves to standing

- Creep on their hands and knees

- Crawl on their belly

- Cruise

By the age of twelve-to-sixteen months, your child typically will be able to

- Turn pages in a book and demonstrate a desire to look at books

- Repeat sounds and words

- Possess an increased bank of receptive language

- Use a shape-sorter and other large puzzles

- Walk independently

For older children, more in-depth testing may be required to identify delays. There are several testing methods available to parents and therapists. If you have a concern about a child's development, obtain an order for therapy. If the child is not displaying appropriate developmental progress for their age based on any of these guidelines, have the child evaluated by a physical, occupational, and speech therapist. All of the therapies overlap in treatments but see the child from a different scientific viewpoint.

Connect with all disciplines if possible, as they all have expertise in different yet overlapping domains. Their expertise reinforces a child's developmental skills. Therapy professionals evaluate a child's individual needs and work with caregivers to create a treatment plan that will best address that child's unique needs.

There are several evaluations available for the therapist and teacher.

1. *Developmental Assessment of Young Children* **test, or the** *DAYC-2*. The *DAYC-2* test is used to identify delays in children between five and eleven years old. It measures the following domains: cognition, communication, physical development, social and emotional development, and adaptive behavior. It was designed to use available materials in the child's natural environment to test for their level of development.

2. *Brigance IED 111*, a comprehensive inventory of early development from birth to seven years old. The skill areas measured include physical development (pre-ambulatory, gross motor, and fine motor), language development, daily living, literacy, mathematics and science, and social-emotional development.

3. *Hawaii Early Learning Profile* or *HELP* is family-centered for infants and toddlers from birth to three years old. *HELP: 3-6* is also available. The format is user-friendly and helps with creating goals and developmentally appropriate activities to be used in therapy. The test can be used upon reevaluation for comparison progress or regression. There are six skill categories observed through play: expressive communication, receptive communication, gross motor, fine motor, social and emotional relation to others, and self-help.

4. *Peabody Development Motor Scale* is a reliable testing device for evaluation and follow-up evaluations. Check to see if your early intervention referral sources will accept these scores for detection and validation of developmental delays and justification of therapy service. The test comes with a kit, which makes the scores more uniformly valid. With rescoring, it also reveals progress on item scores to assist in justifying additional therapy needed or goals met.

Look, Listen, and Feel

Look at the child, environment, and caregivers. Teach the caregivers so there is a support and exercise system daily. Listen and watch to see if the child is neurologically rewiring from the therapy program. Also, listen to see if the parents are overwhelmed or feel the program has empowered them. Try to fit therapeutic activities into their existing daily routines. Feel for high, low, or mixed tone in the child. Determine what speed and duration therapeutic intervention will work to rewire and make their tone more typical. If you are unsure if your patient needs further evaluation, use the following list to check your patient's developmental progress:

1. ***Suck and swallow.*** The child performs suck and swallow well without choking or a rattling sound in their chest, eats enough to get fully satisfied and is growing. Check that the tongue attachment is anterior on the floor of the mouth. Ankyloglossia is when the tongue is "tied"—the short and thick lingual frenulum may interfere with movement of the tongue required in sucking, swallowing, movement of food in the mouth, and speech. Did the infant have a history of intubation? You may want to recommend speech and occupational therapists with special training in swallowing and feeding.

2. ***Visual tracking*** is the ability to follow objects with the eyes—up, down, left, right and near- far. Vision is a powerful tool for rewiring two or more sensory/motor functions. Visual information is combined with sensory information such as touch, taste, smell, and processing memories. Visual tracking relates to the ability to look in different directions—superior, inferior, left, right, convergence, and divergence. This ability is required for quality reading ability, coordination, safety and depth perception. Physical and occupational therapists can receive additional training in vision rehabilitation. If you

feel that the patient is having trouble with visual tracking, eye teaming, convergence, or divergence, begin visual exercises. If the exercises begin *before* age two, progress may be rapid. If started *after* two, progress may be slower.

3. ***Distractibility or focus.*** Determine if the child is able to watch and maintain gaze or attention to you, a toy, book, music, phone, or tablet. Look at the child's surroundings; are they calm and quiet or noisy and chaotic? Consider an evaluation checkup on cranial nerves. Is the patient on medication? Does the patient have a history of neonatal abstinence syndrome? Evaluate to see if the child is having difficulty processing information during particular activities. Break down the activity to see if the patient is able to maintain focus. If the child's mind runs on multiple tracks, as ours often does, try combining activities. This may include having their favorite song playing, putting a puzzle together, and blowing bubbles. Surprisingly, we found that in patients with autism or ADD/ADHD, this kind of combination activity can reign in attention.

4. ***Sensitivity or reactivity*** to touch, sound, or light. If a child experiences a high level of sensitivity to visual or tactile stimulation, things may seem too bright, too loud, or too much for them. Put yourself in the same position as you are placing the child. For example, if the child is supine, look at the ceiling; how are the lights affecting you? Are they shining in your eyes? Is it difficult to see on object held in front of you against the lighted ceiling? If so, the toy, even though brightly colored, will appear as shadowed. You may want to consider using side lamps rather than overhead lighting. Sometimes light or sound can be overpowering to a nervous system and difficult to process.

5. *Fussy with clothing issues.* When it comes to putting on clothes or shoes, a child may fight or refuse to wear certain types or textures of clothing next to their skin. You may utilize additional skills in treating sensory integration issues. Visualize this: another person can tickle you, yet you cannot tickle yourself. A child has more control over dressing, picking out clothing, and delivering their own therapy treatments in home programs. We have some children brush themselves. When they are active on their own treatments, the brain opens additional pathways for sensory and motor feedback loops. This assists neuroplasticity in finding pathways that are patent and functional.

6. *Clumsiness* relates to balance and knowing where a child's body is in space. The eyes, the balance mechanism in the ears, and the sensory feedback of the body in relation to gravity and touch might not functionally communicate with each other. Nervous system integration and communication tell the head, neck, trunk, and extremities where they are in the environment. Vision, head, and neck coordination are the first elements to be controlled in conjunction with visual tracking and the cranial weight maintained against gravity. The trunk and upper and lower extremities follow. This cephal-to-caudal process is also the normal pattern by which sensory stimulation techniques are delivered to the baby, the way *brain files* are stored, and the natural process for incoming information. When delivered in this fashion, the sensory elements are processed more easily and results in therapy sessions are expedient.

   a. Also take note if the **feet are flat**. This indicates that the tibia and femur are positioned in an internal rotation presentation. In standing, the feet may rest wider than the shoulders. This torque of internal rotation is translated throughout the joints of the lower extremities and trunk. It restricts trunk rotation, heel-toe gait, arm swing and competent balance. Dynamic gel supports in shoes will support the feet in a neutral position and unlock rotation.

b. Look at both feet resting on the floor and note if the left and right calcaneus seems to be in valgus. Do the Achilles tendons look like backward parentheses while standing? If so, the arch and heel need support to upright the foot.

c. Is the forefoot pronated? Check to see if the child has an obligatory plantar grasp. Do they have low tone with feet collapsing on the floor? If so, the therapist may need to go back to plan "b" above and support arch and heel.

d. Where is the navicular in relation to the floor?

e. Is the medial malleolus much closer to the floor than the lateral malleolus?

f. Does the child weight shift or walk with little to no rotation of the lower extremities and trunk?

7. *Symmetrical eyes*

a. The eyes should move together in each direction: up, down, right, and left. This is called teaming.

b. Convergence and divergence is the ability for the eyes to move in a relation to an object that is near and far. Depth perception is essential for safety and negotiation of space during mobility.

c. Vision exercises assist in developing these skills. The extraocular muscles are striated and come under voluntary control. I believe these muscles can demonstrate high or low tone as in the body after a brain injury. In our clinic, we have had excellent results treating the tone and tremor of the brain-based innervation of the eye musculature. Ocular neuromyotonia was described as spasm of extraocular muscles in 14 patients.

Ezra, E. Spalton, D. (April 1996). Ocular neuromyotonia. *Br J Ophthalmol.* 350-355. Retrieved 020219.

8. *Symmetrical body features*

   a. Is your patient's head symmetrical and shaped similarly on both sides? Are the ears even? Is the head in midline or does it demonstrate torticollis?

   b. With your evaluation, do both sides of the trunk, arms and legs reveal similar tone qualities, and is range-of-motion full?

   c. Are upper extremities equal in length as well as lower extremities?

   d. Palpate the bony processes and check for symmetry of length and connection to joints.

9. *Gross motor skills*

   a. Does your patient have difficulty with rolling over, coming to sitting, pull to standing, cruising, walking?

   b. Does the patient walk on their toes intermittently or constantly?

   c. Do they grip their toes when you place your finger on the ball of the foot or in barefoot weight bearing as in positive plantar grasp?

d. Do they rise on their toes in standing or walking while looking up and down?

10. *Fine motor skills.* Does the child have trouble with visual tracking, grasping and pinching with her hands, coloring or writing, tying shoes, or buttoning clothing?

11. *Consider history.* Has the child had exposure to medications, drugs or smoking? Many chemicals cross the blood brain barrier of the mother as well as the infant. Any falls or motor vehicle accidents during fetal development?

12. *Reticular Activating System.* This system monitors the fetus, infant, and child to assist in regulation of the nervous system. Smoking during pregnancy can affect a child's pre-attention, attention, and cortical function throughout development. It may also intensify attention dis-regulation throughout the child's life.

In our office we use *ACORN* by this author, to assist in evaluation and treatment options for children. We consider the way a child's brain and body develop. The primary goal is to deliver therapy in an easily assimilated manner for the central nervous system to process and rewire through neuroplasticity techniques.

ACORN

A   Automatic Responses from Subconscious Mind. Realize that the child may not be aware of activity, movement, response, or reflex. Video the patient with permission, then show patient and caregiver the video.

1. Expression on the face reveals mood, fear, happy, content

2. Symmetry of eyebrows, nose, lips, eye alignment, tongue positions may reveal uneven tone in the face, central nervous system signal interruption and disruption in the cranial nerve innervation.

C Conscious. Control, bring body part/movement into consciousness. This requires watching, teaching and learning.

1. Sensory narration of body parts, sensory stimulation techniques such as brushing, tapping, cool temperature

2. Note the relation of active verbal commands, tone of the therapist and changes in motor control

3. Therapist requests activity with vision to follow object and attention to task

4. Situation awareness is the child's perception of knowing what is going on around us.

O Orient. The child is given extra sensational experiences to determine the perimeter of his body, joints as well position in space. This basic information determines how the child relates to objects in the environment. With all activities the child will subconsciously reference - this is my body, this is not.

1. The child will determine position of body or body part in space relative to gravity and safety.

2. Awakening the sensory endings on skin assists the child in determining positional organization of head and neck as well as their hands attached to the arm and body, and feet attached to legs and trunk.

3. Stimulation of proprioceptors in trunk, upper and lower extremity joints assists the central nervous system in knowing the feel of weight bearing activities.

4. When the child is able to realize a body part/body, they will then move it more successfully and in a functional motion in their environment.

5. These treatments will improve awareness of protective responses and balance in sitting, crawling, standing and ambulation.

R   Rewire. Neuroplasticity - Primitive reflex pattern – There are multiple methods to integrate primitive reflexes and increase functional motor movements. To re-pattern a primitive reflex; allow the child to move into the reflex pattern, then attract eyes to move with visual tracking light/object/rattle/face opposite direction of the pattern. This decreases the strength of the primitive reflex.

1. Gently hold the rest of the body still as the head turns, extends, or flexes.

2. Fatigue reflex – repeat, repeat, repeat eye movements, and stimulate skin nerve endings toward numbness. This will make the patterns less reactive.

3. Stimulate the body, hands, and feet to *numb and dumb* the sensory receptors.

4. For tremor reduction, use intense vibration. *Like treats like* in the natural health world. This is performed over specific areas for success.

5. To change tone one must send sensation into the nervous system. To treat high tone fatigue spasticity by overstimulation with brushing or vibration. To treat low tone, short duration of intense stimulation will improve tone quality.

6. For increasing functional movement and strength use a higher-level cognitive task for the brain to rely on cortex connections rather than lower-brain centers.

7. Seminars by this author are available to learn additional skills.

N   Neuroplasticity Exercises are specific and need to be practiced at home daily.

1. Wake up the nervous system with short duration of sensory experiences.

2. Stimulate primary senses such as smell, vision, hearing and touch.

3. Specific stimulation for increased or decreased tone.

4. Parents observe, practice, repeat and gain feedback from the therapist.

5. Therapist to load automatic actions in lower-brain centers with new information which will regulate tone and motor function.

6. Practicing activities places movements in subconscious.

7. Children are able to attend to higher-level skills when neuroplasticity has assisted in lowering high tone, increasing tone in lower-tone individuals, and placing primitive reflexes in the background.

8. The child will be able to accomplish more multiple-step directions when balance and tone are in the subconscious mind.

Treatment Techniques

1. 3-D sensation – Stimulate head, neck, trunk, upper and lower extremities with brisk fast hand rubbing similar to massage techniques. Hands need to stay in contact with

skin surfaces. (avoid mouth and under diaper areas due to high population of nerve endings)

2. Brain exercises – By pairing two activities, such as light and sound, or sensation and motion, the brain will fire these together and connect the signals. The neural conduction will seek a patent pathway as well as form new connections.

3. Crossing the hemispheres with activities involves crossing midline with vision, sensation, hands, feet, neck and trunk rotation.

4. Rock, roll, and swing are the different directions of the semicircular canals. They are at right angles to each other. Taking a child through the motions will stimulate all of the semicircular canals and assist with eye motion and balance control. Moving a head in a yes motion is *Rock*. The no motion is *Roll*. The head in a swing laterally toward the shoulders is *Swing*.

5. Visual tracking is performed with a light and sound together. Up, down, left, right, near to far motions.

6. Light, sound move eyes/head up-down or left-right to change reflex/response is used to fatigue the primitive reflex patterns so as to free more voluntary movements.

7. Adding music increases the activity of the limbic system and touches all of the lobes from the interior. Similar to a subway that can take you across town, the limbic system can deliver sensory information to different parts of the central nervous system with or without a corpus callosum.

8. Prolonged stimulation will numb and dumb high tone so as not to overpower voluntary movement.

9. Simulation for short duration will increase tone. Keep in mind you just want to wake up the nervous system with this technique.

Subconscious Mind

What reactions of your patient are below the level of consciousness? What lives in the subconscious? What do you not think about that occurs anyway?

1. Tone

2. Primitive reflexes

3. Responses – balance

4. Practiced movements – typing

5. Activities one can do when distracted or automatically

   a. Get dressed

   b. Put keys somewhere

   c. Drive car

   d. Play musical instrument

   e. Turn pages of a book

   f. Eat

When you can change the placement of connecting functions in the brain, you can change the neurological level and type of function. One can *refine movements* as well as *change tone and tremor*. In natural health, "like treats like," and before- and after-video documentation has verified the use of vibration to decrease tremors. Use graph paper for drawing a square, circle and triangle.

This practice is simple documentation and the patient can keep the before and after treatment results. The patient that is able to see immediate results is a compliant patient.

Awareness is in the present time and is the perception of an event, person, emotion, sensation, or object. We are able to analyze these reactions on a subconscious and/or conscious level and determine if they are beneficial, safe, or negative. It can be for an internal or external perception (visceral or sensory). Body language of an encounter with an individual will begin a receptive response or a fight-or-flight response.

According to Patryk and Kasia Wezoqski in their book *Without Saying a Word (2018)*, body language is a patient-specific concept and may trigger subconscious or conscious processing. A patient's body will always want to tell the truth about what they are feeling about their situation and you talking to them. This can make a big difference in your patient's learning and remembering home programs. Does you patient react differently if you wear street clothing instead of scrubs? This may be especially true if the child spent time in NICU, PICU, or the hospital experiencing procedures. What do the caregivers body positions tell you about their receptiveness and interaction with the therapist, the therapy program and home exercises?

Basic awareness of internal and external worlds may lie in the brain stem according to Bjorn Merker. He studied several children who were missing 80 percent of their brain. Consciousness in the Raw, *Science News Online,* September 2007.. Subconscious awareness drives responses to gravity changes, balance in sitting, standing, walking, and running. Improved body control and attainment of milestones can be brought into conscious awareness with the help of a skilled therapist.

Conscious awareness relates to more cortical involvement uses a higher level processing in the brain. Learning new skills demands conscious learning initially, and with repeated practice may become a subconscious action. Individuals performing music, driving, diving, or a marathon run may think other thoughts while doing these activities. Therapists may suggest alterations on practiced activities such as gait pattern (walk forward, backward, sideways, on foam or uneven ground) to bring the activity to the cortex and thinking brain. Small alterations of a skill can bring the movements into more conscious awareness.

Are You Ready to Play?

COMPASS Program

It is important to remember how the various areas of the brain are connected to each other. When all areas of the nervous system are working together, the brain can receive information, integrate stimuli, make sense of the world, and respond appropriately. The nervous system and connections need to be in place for all the developmental skills to surface and to be accomplished. Most children with challenges have brain changes that affect motor skills. We, as therapists, need to address the cause of movement disorders in the central nervous system in order to make positive headway in the child's attainment of motor milestones.

We are looking at causes as well as symptoms; we attend to both. If only symptoms are treated, the causes will persist if they are not addressed. If activities are incorporated that also stimulate the primary connections and brain (i.e., nervous system development), progress is rapid related to motor skills. These activities will help connect the nervous system so it works better and more efficiently.

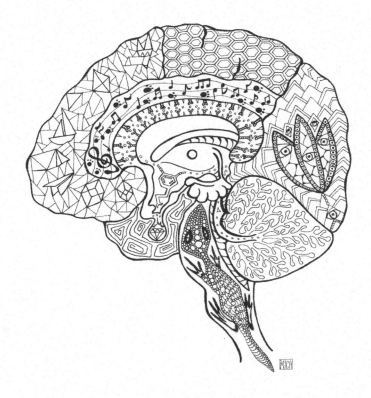

COMPASS Program for infants and toddlers

A. Evaluate *where* in the nervous system the patient has functional pathways.

B. Determine *what* areas of the central nervous system are not working well.

C. Combine properties of these findings through sensation to *wire* them together.

D. *When* the pathways are used frequently the connections will thrive and motor function will increase.

1. Ten Fingers and Ten Toes

Hand delivered sensation on the face, neck, trunk, arms, and legs from manual techniques with use of a brush, hands, or inside out sock, tells babies where their bodies are in space. Gently briskly rub the head, neck, trunk, arms, hands, legs, and feet while narrating the body part being touched. Children with high tone will need longer stimulation to "numb and dumb" the body parts. Spasticity is sensory driven; once sensation is over-stimulated, the primitive reflexes become less reactive and get out of the way of voluntary movements. The child with low tone requires quick and short stimulation to "wake up" the sensory endings.

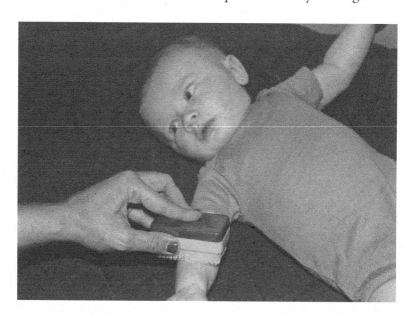

2. Bright Baby Eyes

Now you know that 30 percent of your cranial nerves are involved in eye movement and that 80 percent of the central nervous system serves or connects to visual functions. Vision is a very powerful force in rewiring the central nervous system for advancing function. Following objects with their eyes is one of the first rotational movements as well as an activity babies can master. An exercise that is fun and helps your baby develop visual abilities is to have them watch and track a favorite toy as you move it in a pattern. Note if the eyes are aligned. Use of the following exercises will help with alignment and 3 dimensional vision.

3. *Visual tracking*

Attract and engage the baby's eyes by using a light wand or shiny toy. Move the object up and down, left and right, near and far, followed by diagonal patterns to strengthen the eye muscles control and focus. Adding sound to a slowly moving object helps with stereoscopic vision and hearing. This also develops wiring for vision and hearing together. The Hebb principle is "Whatever fires together, wires together."

All movements are led by the eyes initially. Rolling is a good example. Rotation of the eyes, neck, then trunk is the sequence of events required for rolling, coming to sitting, and effective ambulation. Rotation is essential to movements and balance.

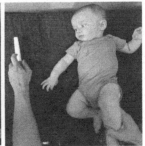

In our clinic, the results of a ten-year study showed that starting these exercises when a child is an infant will help them increase reading ability, depth perception, and coordination in everyday activities and sports as they grow. Speeding up coordination and integration of vision ultimately helps with overall brain development and learning.

Movement of the eyes can influence primitive reflex patterns. Superior eye direction is also the initiator of neck extension. I refer to this as the *nose up–toes up* posture. Exercising the *nose up–toes up* posture can increase elicitation of the Moro and Labyrinthine reflexes, increasing extension postures in the child. This is also a characteristic of some children who walk on their toes; most all of their eye targets are higher than their eye level. When they look up, it brings their body into more of an extension pattern. This is demonstrated from nose to toes. Lower the eye targets, and see if the child starts utilizing more of a heel-toe gait pattern.

When you want to decrease toe walking and the extension influence on posture, lower the child's eye gaze onto a visual target at or below the neutral sight line (i.e., using a tablet, light, toy, etc.). Objects of interest lowered in this fashion at home and in the classroom promote decreased frequency of toe walking. Follow by re-evaluating the child's posture and control with the lower eye gaze. Continued influence by primitive reflexes, which live in the lower-brain centers, will rob a child of balance control and active motor movements.

Another technique that assists in integration of plantar grasp is desensitization with prolonged stimulation with brush, vibrator, or inside-out sock. Plantar grasp is driven by sensory stimulation of the ball of the foot, under the metatarsal heads. The toes curl downward and the foot plantar flexes in response to pressure.

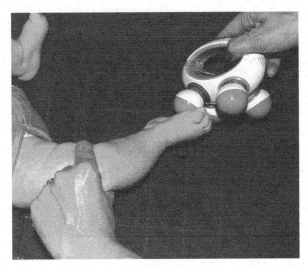

Also evaluate the Achilles length and gastroc soleus length while the child is in hip and knee flexion. This will reduce the influence of extension in the primitive reflex pattern synergies. If a brace is required, consider use of splinting (AFO) at night only. The child may demonstrate little to no spasticity while asleep, and the stretch to twenty degrees dorsiflexion will be easier to accomplish.

Consider on-off approach to bracing. If constantly braced, the body is robbed of sensory experiences that drive brain connections and learning. The feet need sensory experiences to integrate primitive reflexes. Sensory experiences, in the awake child, are required to process weight bearing proprioception, balance, and visual information. In the foot there are 26 bones, 30 joints, and more than 100 muscles, ligaments, and tendons. Movement of the bones and joints, and more of the foot with weight shifting assists in developing strength to the lower extremity musculature, bone density, and tensile stability and strength of the supporting ligaments.

4. *Rock, Roll, and Swing*

Rocking, rolling, and swinging your baby uses multiple senses and can help the child identify where they are in space. The vestibular system and visual system are closely connected. In the brain, they are next-door neighbors. Securely hold the child and support their head. Use fast motions with shorter duration to increase tone in children with lower tone qualities. Adding rather sudden stops helps babies to sense changes in motion and direction. Slow movements of longer duration can be relaxing, calming, and place higher tone children into a state of lower-tone effects.

All head movements stimulate the semicircular canal motion detectors in the ears, which are set at right angles to each other—kind of like your own gyroscope. The different movements are more easily understood by thinking of moving your head in *yes, no,* and *I don't know* movements (ear to shoulder on each side).

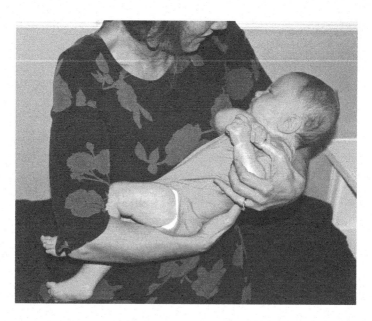

5. *Two Eyes and Two Ears*

Stimulation of eyes and ears with light and sound sends signals directly to the brain. One of the baby's initial movements is to cross midline using eye rotation. Location of a light being tapped by the practitioner's finger draws the child in to use the eye/ear functions. The stronger connection is stimulated and may cross-connect the weaker function because of neuroplasticity wiring mechanisms.

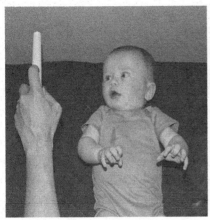 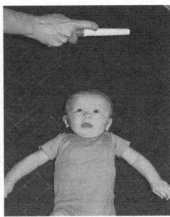

The neural connections from the eyes and ears to the brain are very short and can cause quick responses. In addition, the visual and auditory receptors within the brain send signals that travel side to side as well as up and down the central nervous system pathways. This paves the way for other neural information traveling from the body and spinal cord to the brain to connect, process, and integrate understanding for motor reactions. The incoming sensory information has connections between the right and left sides of the brain. If there is difficulty in processing information, the brain will rewire itself when given specific sensory information. This is the essence of neuroplasticity.

Stimulate the right and left vision and hearing fields individually and then together to coordinate stereoscopic location ability of eyes and ears. A variation of peek-a-boo is an example of a game you can play with your baby that would engage both the eyes and ears. Activities involving the right eye and ear send information to specific areas of the brain. This exercise is followed by using the left eye and ear.

Activities that stimulate both sides together engage crossover connections between both sides of the brain. Most people develop a dominant side in the perception of sight and sound, just like developing right- or left-handedness. However, regardless of which side becomes dominant, these crossover exercises increase a child's abilities to look and listen more effectively. Integrate sound into the visual stimulation exercises. Place your hand over one of the child's ears while talking to the baby to vary the information going to the brain.

When emotion from the practitioner is added into this mix during visual and auditory tracking, the limbic system is activated. The limbic system sends emotionally charged information to all of the lobes in the cortex from the undersurface of the cortical layers. This is a useful tool when treating a child with agenesis of the corpus callosum or damage to central brain structures. Again, visual tracking is one of the first rotary movements accomplished for crossing midline. Eye movement leads the head and neck to turn before trunk movements occur. As we remember in proprioceptive neuromuscular facilitation, rotation is essential to all movements.

6. *Power of Motion – Rotation*

Rotation is essential to starting and stopping coordinated voluntary motions. All motions have a rotational component although they may appear slight. Every motion has an equal and opposite movement: up and down; in and out; right and left. If rotation is eliminated because of brain challenges in the cortex and midbrain structures, all motions will be limited in function. Movement of eyes, head, neck, and trunk is the beginning of early motion in the baby and child, and all begin with a rotation.

Starting with visual tracking and head/neck rotation, the trunk rotates to promote rolling. Rotation is key in coming to sitting. It is my personal belief that coming to sit and maintaining sitting is one of the hardest motor skills for a child. Once that is accomplished, most of the following skills are much easier because they build on fundamental neural connections related to movements required for sitting.

Rotation initiates movements. Gently rolling the trunk, arms, and legs similarly to rolling play dough helps a baby gain voluntary motions. Exercises that focus on strength as well as stretching in all ranges of motion set the stage for more complicated movements later as a child and adult. Babies must learn to reach and grasp, feed themselves, and play with toys.

When we look at the musculature, where can we find straight-line pulls? Power and force come into play with the muscular attachments that demonstrate rotation as we move. When you observe the musculature of the face, note the angles and rotary ability of the contraction and relaxation phases. Expression, eye and mouth open and closure are accomplished with muscles that have rotary components. Manual therapy to the face follows the layers of muscular formations and rotary qualities.

Let us look forward in age at the patient with Parkinson's disease. They demonstrate "masked face" and have difficulty starting and stopping their gait. If we look further, they have lost rotational abilities. Some of the children we treat have also lost rotation and may demonstrate the above symptoms. Damage to the cerebellum, substantia nigra, basal ganglia, or the nervous system connections related to these areas may have an effect on rotary movements in motor components. This will affect starting and stopping gait and balance. Sometimes walkers rob our children of rotation during gait. Make adjustments to the walker or gait trainer to allow rotation; otherwise, the child will likely demonstrate a side-to-side stiff gait pattern with deficient balance abilities.

7. *Proprioception*

The stimulation of proprioceptors is an inside job. It lies within the joints. *Joint tap* the baby's elbow while driving proprioception toward the shoulder. Tap their hand while their elbow is extended. Tap their knee while flexed to drive information into the hip proprioceptors. Then tap the heel with their leg in a straightened position. This will teach the joint proprioceptors, help with coordination, and emphasize how the body reacts to weight bearing, motion, and space around them.

While the baby is in a four-point position (on their hands and knees), tap them on the shoulder then over the hip toward the floor. This will help them recognize weight-bearing and assist the nervous system in supportive control.

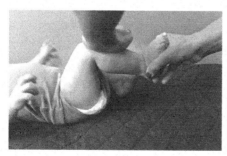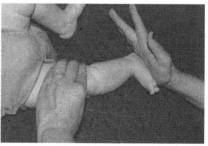

Support the baby's trunk with your hands in front and back while the child is in a sitting position on your knee. We describe it to parents as the child being in a sandwich. Run your fingers along the paraspinals to aid in contracting the muscles. Run your fingertips from the top of the chest down the tummy to contract and strengthen the stomach muscles.

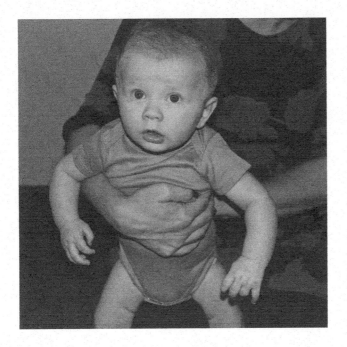

These activities increase proprioception in the spine, core strength, posture, and erect sitting control. We briefly stimulate the abdomen, similarly to how the parent washes the trunk. The child needs to realize they have a three-dimensional core. Their realization of this fact allows improved stability and use of motor skills. Gently bouncing the baby on the therapists thigh will also stimulate proprioceptors in the spine.

8. *Hold On and Let Go*

Mastering motion of the arms and hands allows babies to reach out, play with toys, and begin to feed themselves. One of the triggers for the grasp reflex of the hand is located on the palm of the hand. Long sleeves can constantly stimulate this pattern, causing the hands to stay fisted. In such cases, the sleeves should be rolled up so they are not touching the hands or wrists.

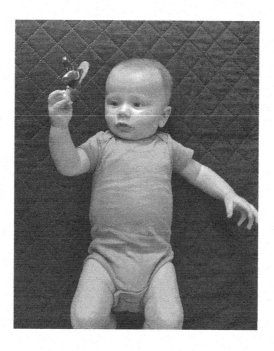

Touching with a finger or an object to the palm will usually cause the baby to close the hand into a fist. If the baby has a problem with high or low tone, rub the neck, shoulder girdle, arm, and hand in a three-dimensional fashion so they are aware they have an arm. If the child has difficulty letting go of an object, stimulate the object with a vibrator to "numb and dumb" the hand. It will then be much easier to gently open the hand and pull the thumb and fingertips away from the object while trying not to touch the palm of the hand. When this is repeated at home by the family, the child will integrate a palmar grasp and have the hands more open to receive incoming sensations.

You may also need to rub or brush the arm, forearm, and the hand vigorously or hold the fingertips and slowly open the hand. Once the hand opens, you can brush, vibrate, or massage in an act to desensitize the palm of the hand, after which the baby will be able to voluntarily open the hand more easily.

The grasp reflex of the hand and foot usually diminishes after six to nine months as the baby begins to make controlled movements to grasp objects, feed themselves, and make early attempts at walking. After this time, if the baby will not release an object from their grasp easily, they may have residual palmar grasp reflex. Some signs that a baby or child may still have plantar grasp include difficulty with putting on their shoes, balance in walking, and toe walking. If the reflex persists, it can be successfully treated with therapy.

9. *Rhymes with Tummy Time*

Floor activities and tummy time are important exercises for the neck and trunk muscles and help develop the natural curves of the spine. These motions prepare the baby for rolling, crawling, and sitting. Rolling requires typical tone on bilateral sides of the trunk, and strength and control of the eyes, neck, and trunk.

While lying on their belly, the baby will practice raising their head, which strengthens the neck and clears the airway for breathing. Pushing up on arms and hands will strengthen their shoulder girdle, arm, and trunk muscles. Tummy time is not always easy, so be patient and remember to take a break when needed. Singing, rhyming, and talking to the baby from different directions—in front and to the right and left—will help them explore new movements and integrate primitive reflexes. Practice and movements inform the midbrain and cortex, primitive reflex forms of movement are no longer needed.

If the baby has a feeding tube, try laying the baby initially on the parent for tummy time. One-inch foam with a hole cut as an opening for the tube creates negative pressure over the tube, and the baby will be more comfortable in a prone position. A similar foam canal can be made for the child with a tracheostomy tube. In our clinic, we use foam to promote agitation-free and pain-free therapy sessions.

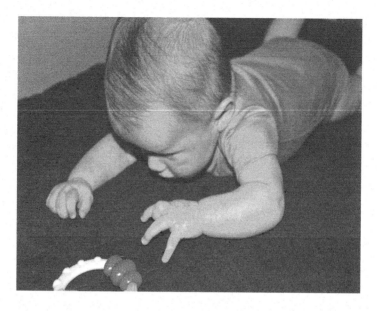

10. Rolling Over

The phrase "watch where you're going!" is literally true because the head and body follow the course that the eyes set as the target. Babies generally initiate turning and rolling over by moving their eyes first, followed by the head, neck, and trunk.

One way to encourage head movement is by attracting the baby's eyes with colorful or black-and-white objects in dynamic movement within their field of vision. This type of stimulation helps with balance, coordination, and movement of the eyes and head.

If there is delay in rolling over, you can catch your baby's attention with an object, starting about one foot in front of their face. Next, bring the object with light and sound, around to the floor on one side of the body. This will help with turning the neck followed by the trunk. You can also bring one knee across the body to touch the floor to help with turning over.

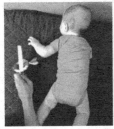

It is important that the baby be able to move their neck and trunk independently from each other. This motion is key for rolling over, coming to a sitting position, pulling to standing, and walking balance. Caution: I do not recommend using a towel or blanket to pull the baby over. The justification for this is, the baby's nervous system will feel like they are falling and will elicit primitive protective responses. This is opposite of what you want to occur.

11. Grrr...Ate

What is the baby eating and drinking? Quality nutrition is essential for the baby to function with good strength and energy. If the baby is congested, coughing, vomiting, or has a runny nose or trouble with breathing, consider talking to your medical professionals and switching the type of milk you use. You may need to do additional research on information for nutritional guidelines for infants and children. Good nutrition is necessary for brain and general development. I am a personal advocate of breast milk.

To assist the baby in holding their bottle as well as continuing to suckle, gently tap the bottom of the bottle and hold the baby's arm at the elbow. Holding at the bony prominence will not confuse the incoming sensation of the arm.

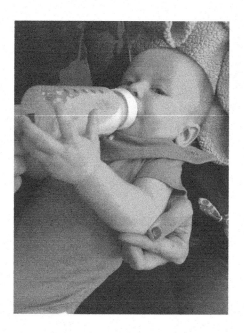

Consider this…nourishment assists in growth of the body and the brain. If the child cannot digest what they ingest, they will not grow or develop needed brain connections. Some of the children we treat may have lost gut bacteria; in those cases probiotics may be necessary to break down food elements in order to obtain the needed vitamins, minerals, amino acids, and enzymes. Talk to the physician or nutritionist.

If a child is tube fed and their age is comparable to children who would eat food, consider blending their food for tube feeding. Contact a specialized nutritionist and/or physician specializing in nutrition of children. Several books are also available on this topic. One example of an excellent book for children is *Homemade Blended Formula Handbook* by Marsha Klein MEd, OTR, and Suzanne Morris Ph.D.. CCC-SLP. Together these clinicians have over 90 years experience. Please research this topic for the latest evidence-based information available.

12. Hand to Mouth

"Crossing midline" means reaching across the center of the body or face. The first motor skill in crossing midline is visual. Eyes are the first to cross midline; they lead the head, neck, and trunk in accomplishing motor skills. When one hand touches the other, both sides of the brain are involved in identifying sensation and location of the hands.

This is also the case when both feet touch each other. Using the hands to play with the feet ipsilateral and contralateral also helps with flexibility (rotation, flexion, and extension) of the trunk. Movement of the trunk in coordination with hand and foot engagement aids in turning over, crawling, creeping, rising from the floor, and balance in sitting and standing.

Children are also learning about their three-dimensional worlds. As they pick up a toy, they have fingers touching two sides of an object, and when they bring that toy to their mouth, they touch a third side. This activity is also multisensory in that smell and taste are involved.

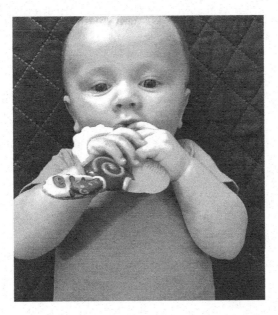

13. Ten Fingers, Ten Toes: What Every Parent Needs to Know

Like the old children's song, "The arm bone is connected to the hand bone...," the nervous system is connected to every organ, tissue, and cell in your body. Everything is connected to everything else. Even when there are challenges with a child, neuroplasticity will allow rewiring to occur around the damaged areas.

Emotions are a great way to engage the child because emotion connects to both sides of the brain. It crosses the hemispheres and aids in integration when combined with additional motor skills. The frontal lobe picks up emotionally charged information. The "emotional brain" limbic system touches each lobe from inside the cortex. Emotion combined with activities is an effective method of enhancing and activating functioning pathways. Use of emotion, sensation, and motor activity combination enhances neuronal pathway connections and wires around damage. This serves to use neuroplasticity to the child's advantage.

Emotion can be added to activities by changing how you verbally or emotionally interact with the child via facial expression and/or tone of voice while exercising with them. For instance, changing your facial expression from gloomy to excited or using a dynamic, sing-song tone of voice while interacting with the baby will create an emotional connection between the exercise and their limbic system.

Your focused attention is important. Children can sense if you are distracted or entirely interested and focused on them. Narrate what you are doing and what they are doing, and name objects. Becoming their narrator will pique their interest in a world with meaning and reasons.

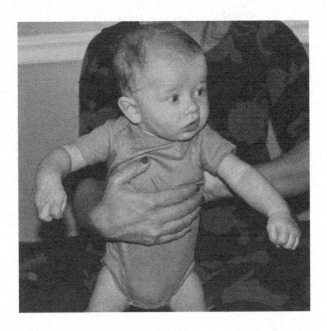

Core strength and stability is essential for movement and use of the hands and feet. If the baby's arms and legs seem weak or uncoordinated, work on rotation and strengthening the neck, trunk, shoulders, and hips. The child can only be as strong as their base of support can manage. Strengthening the neck and trunk can support the arms and legs, increasing functional abilities.

Tone lives in the brain and strength in the muscles.

When babies need help, they can't wait for it. The sooner a treatment begins, the quicker changes happen. When tone qualities are more typical/normal, the child can move their body in space, walk, play, and engage with activities. When their tone is more typical, that is the time to increase strength. Find toys that have weight or make them from recycled single-use baby bottles, and give them to the babies to lift or move around with their hands or feet. Be sure you tape the tops on the bottles so they cannot open them. Balls or toys that are filled with sand or water work well.

Make sure the baby can get their tiny hands around whatever toys you give them. Have them reach out, up, and across their bodies to get the toy. This will increase strength and motion of shoulders and arms. Babies will continue as long as you can make it fun or until they get tired.

In our clinic, we have children lift one- to two-pound weighted toys that make noise like a rattle. The children shake, rattle, and sometimes roll back and forth to play with them. If they do this one hundred times, it may equal one hundred to two hundred pounds of work. The more fun you make it, the more they will work. Children will play longer than they will work. So will we.

14. Parts of the Brain that "Fire Together, Wire Together" Hebb principle

Have you ever heard a song or smelled a fragrance that reminded you of a place or scenario from your past? That is because your brain has its own patterns for remembering through motions, emotions, and our senses of sound, taste, sight, and smell. Combining two functions in the brain can help "wire them together." The NIH printed an article relating to the sense of smell and stimulation of stem cells in 2014. The article is titled *Scientists Sniff Out Unexpected Role for Stem Cells in the Brain* by Leonardo Belluscio PhD. From the NIH's National Institute of Neurological Disorders and Stroke (NINDS).

Using a variety of adjectives with activities stimulates different parts of the brain. *Smelling* a *small, soft, yellow* flower activity for the baby, narrated by the adult is just one example. This process helps the child categorize, associate, retrieve, and use the information they collect to understand the world around them. This exercise also helps them to learn colors, size, shape, categories, location, and direction early on.

15. Lucky Love of Music

Music is a great tool for learning. Most, if not all, of us learned our ABCs and 123s to the rhythm of a song. Music can also increase coordinated movements by incorporating rhythm with clapping, singing, and dancing. The *limbic system* is the "emotional brain" and is stimulated by music because of music's emotional content and fun nature.

Musical activities stimulate the whole brain, especially the frontal cortex of the brain. This area of the brain is responsible for learning rhythmic skills such as typing, playing the piano, and writing words. Music and beats perceived in the auditory system send stimulation that reaches into the spinal cord upward on brain stem, subcortical, and cortical levels. This changes function in sensorimotor cortex, inferior frontal gyrus, and the cerebellum.

Music and beats also assist in crawling and gait. The musical beats go deep into the brain, since music possesses emotional components. The influences of exercises set to music are spread deep through the limbic system, which connects to all the cortical lobes from the inside. This addition of emotional components, music, and beats brings in the brain stem, midbrain, and cerebrum functions, causing connections to pathways that are functional.

16. Heavenly Rest

Relaxation is as important as exercise. Quality rest is essential for the brain to record and categorize memories of daily activities and to restore mental vitality, which is necessary for sending information into the proper pathways of the nervous system. We always think the elephant never forgets, but in this circumstance, the hippo (hippocampus) is involved in processing the events of the day before and storing them as memories.

In the book *Why We Sleep*, author Matthew Walker (2017), explains that rapid eye movement (REM) sleep is very important in memory processing. This occurs in conjunction with coordination of the central nervous system, cerebrum, and hippocampus. Loss of sleep is directly connected to irregular sleep patterns and loss of memory, including difficulty remembering skills and words.

If a child is on medication, has seizures during sleep, or has brain stem damage that affects sleep patterns, memory will most likely be affected. When memory is affected, learning and motor skills will also be delayed. Paying special attention to remedying sleep patterns will assist the child in retaining memories as well as learning motor skills.

If a child or caregiver is in fight-or-flight mode, it is difficult for them to listen to the medical professional and attend to home exercises. In our experience, it is essential to provide an environment to decrease stress, increase education, and hand out hope with a reasonable plan for goal attainment. A reduced distraction environment for therapy sessions is important. Massage, exercise, and educated play will assure better relaxation and deeper sleep. Teaching the caregivers will empower them, and the child will be the beneficiary.

17. *What a Pacifier Can Do*

For babies with tongue protrusion, weak muscles, difficulty with sucking and swallowing, or poor tone or mouth closure, a pacifier can be a great instrument. The force of sucking, swallowing, tongue movements, and closing the mouth associated with active pacifier use makes it a powerful tool that can help with developing some of the speech muscles later. It also increases general head and neck control and decreases drooling. Babies born with Down syndrome or low tone are good candidates for pacifier therapy.

Open your own mouth and try to swallow. One can not swallow unless the mouth is closed and the tongue is able to travel to the roof of the mouth to assure epiglottis closure. Being able to close the mouth for swallowing reduces the risk of aspiration. Brisk massage to the side of the baby's head and jaws over the temporalis and masseter muscles can increase muscle tone and control for closure of the mouth and ability to swallow. Referral to feeding therapy may also be in the best interest of the child and family.

18. *Speech*

One way to improve the baby's receptive speech development is to talk slowly in front of them. Talking onto their cheek allows them to feel the changes in pressure during speech. Lightly press your lips to your baby's cheek, and say words starting with b, d, or m, *ball, dada, mama*. Make an "oo" sound like boo, poo, moo. Combine that with talking on one side of the face to excite one ear and one eye, and then repeat on the other side, as we've done in earlier exercises.

Wait for the baby's response before proceeding to the next exercise. It may take longer for the baby to respond to this exercise, as it uses a longer route through the brain to learn, process, and reproduce a sound initially. With repetition and practice, the response will come more quickly.

Multisensory experiences can serve to rewire around compromised areas and provide detours along alternate pathways. Sensation of the caregiver speaking on the cheek connects to the sound and thus goes into the baby's brain via cranial nerves.

Next speak facing the child, slowly at first so they can see your tongue, lips, and teeth positions with the use of words. The cranial nerves are fast fibers in close proximity to the brain lobes that serve to interconnect for language in the temporal lobes. Use of emotion while talking to the child will also connect to the limbic system and find neural tissue that is viable. New dendrites are fed by use and novel activities.

19. *Communication of Touch*

You can use massage to "reduce high tone response" or to "wake up" your baby's nervous system. As therapists, we actually contribute to the sensory system learning of the child. They perform motor skills and through feedback loops and our sensory assistance, change to motor patterns that prove more successful. When we move a baby's arm to help with protective response in sitting, their nervous system detects our hands touching their body and arm, and proprioceptors detect weight and pull of gravity on joints. Hold to carpals and condyles.

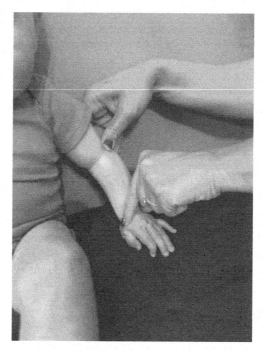

We only have power over a child's sensory components in treatments. If you are not getting motor movements desired, change the sensory information going into a child's nervous system. For example, change your hand placement; instead of holding to muscles and long bones, place your hand over the joints. The feedback loops—sensation to motor skills and back to sensation—and correction of motor skill are part of the saving grace in therapy sessions. This is also the ideology we utilize in correction of a child's gross or fine motor skill.

To help a child relax and/or decrease tone, massage them slowly with gentle, long, and even strokes (avoid mouth and diaper areas because of the intense number of nerve endings). Use slow massage on the baby's head and neck. "Numb and dumb" the sensory receptors because primitive reflexes are driven by sensory experiences. If the tissues are repeatedly stimulated, they will tune out the information. (This is similar to having the radio on constantly and you forget it is playing.)

When the tone is reduced, strength will show up. Strength lives in the muscles, and tone lives in the brain. Tone is monitored by the reticular formation, which is a sensory monitor. Feedback loops change motor tone responses to become more appropriate.

We need to be reminded of the realization that tone comes from the brain. Bracing a child's body makes them look like they are standing, but reliance on bracing does not increase the strength of the child's position, ligaments, or tendons. Therapeutic techniques should send information to the central nervous system to re-regulate the child's tone, which will allow them to catch up closer to the monthly milestone measures.

To wake up a child's nervous system and increase their tone, massage the child quickly with brisk strokes for a short duration. Start each session by massaging the head and neck, then moving to the trunk, arms to hands, and, finally, legs to feet. This is the same way a baby develops. The central nervous system's filing order will understand this delivery of exercises easily.

Name all the child's body parts as you touch and massage them. They will learn their arms and legs, hands, fingernails, teeth, lips, and so on. When they are older and draw a picture of themselves, they may draw more body parts than their peers, such as eyelashes and fingernails. In our clinic, children with low vision or blindness have increased balance and coordination. The child will know their orientation in space which is imperative for effective movement in the environment.

20. Shaking Sticks

A vibrating massage tool—battery-operated or plug-in—can increase or decrease sensitivity of parts of the body. To increase tone, quickly move the tool over the back of the neck, down the back, around the chest and tummy, arms to hands, then legs to feet. This serves to stimulate muscle contractions and tone. On the other hand, holding the tool in one place—over the palm of the hand or the ball of the foot, for example—can help reduce the grasp reflex and have a desensitizing, numbing effect.

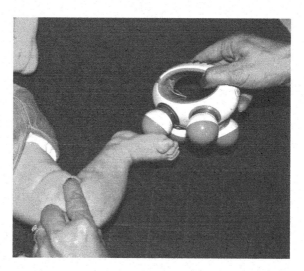

With a vibrator's power, avoid using the massage tool around the mouth and diaper area, as these have a large number of nerve fibers and may overload the nervous system. This may lead to seizures in a seizure-prone child. Speech and Occupational Therapists have special qualifications and vibrators for use around and in the mouth to advance feeding and speaking skills. Sensation is key in changing all motor movements whether they are involuntary or voluntary.

Sensory Stimulation for Neuroplasticity

The only modality we have control over as therapists is sensation. Therapists can assist in directing motions, skills, and motor milestone accomplishments. If you feel the child's fine or gross motor demonstration of movement is not functional, change the sensory stimulation and hand placement guidance. Through sensory-motor feedback loops, the child will correct their motor skills.

Vibration, the sensation of cool temperature, pressure, brushing, tapping, stretching, weightlessness, and compression all excite different nerve endings and make muscles ready for action and movement. Cooling tools used on a child over six months in age—applied in a quick swiping motion over muscles—can excite them and wake up tone. Warmth from a bath will soothe and relax muscles.

Cooling sensations, brushing, tapping, weight-bearing on joints, and stretching can also excite muscles and increase tone. Use of tilt in sitting, kneeling and standing is a quick movement. If performed slowly, it will not trigger the protective response. These sensory stimulation techniques advance babies' sense of their own bodies and how to coordinate their bodies by giving sensory feedback about where they are in space.

Children presenting with hemi-spasticity will often have an arm that is flexed with the hand clasped closed while their lower extremities may present in extension. We also need to pay particular attention to the neck and trunk as this higher tone will restrict the primary movement of rotation. This will resemble an Asymmetrical Tonic Neck Response (ASTNR) pattern, and can also affect neck, trunk, upper and lower extremity with higher tone qualities.

ASTNR may have its overwhelming power decreased by diverting the eye attention to the opposite lateral direction. This movement of the eyes releases the flexion/extension synergies on the affected side of the body. This then allows treatment through purposeful overstimulation to the affected neck, trunk, and upper and lower extremities with a vibrator or brush in a three-dimensional fashion to decrease sensation. *Numbing and dumbing* decreases spastic tone and permits more active movements.

Conclusion

As you do the therapeutic activities listed in this book with your patients, you will experience the program helping them develop faster, learn more, and get a real head start on life.

In my physical therapy practice over a forty-year period, I have seen amazing advances happen, and you can too. When you demonstrate a caring attitude, compassion, and make a real connection with the children in your care, changes will happen right in front of your eyes. We obtain photo and video releases from our parents. You may see advanced results in a single visit. We all know you cannot go back in time. If you also video in slow motion, you can pick apart the components to address in the therapy sessions to assist parent and child in skill attainment.

It is my mission to educate interested individuals in neuroplasticity techniques who have direct contact with babies and children, especially those patients with developmental delays. We teach all individuals in contact with the child.

By being aware of the unique challenges delayed children face, we have a greater opportunity to promote development and to help connect the multiple functions of the mind. The primary goal of this book is to bring information directly to therapists and to avoid the pitfalls of delayed diagnosis and treatment. I want to educate therapists and caregivers to help the patient progress development and skills, no matter what the challenges may be.

To quote *The Florence Prescription* by Joe Tye (2014) "You can never listen too much or talk too little." Rehabilitation is all about a patient-parent-therapist connection; it is a three-legged stool. If one leg is removed, the whole thing falls down. When a therapist listens to the patient and caregiver, only then can they give insightful information and offer coordinated pathways to attain mutual goals of development and recovery. Together, we can make a positive difference that will last a lifetime.

To contact me, please use email. I answer all emails, so if you do not receive a reply, I may not have received it. Try again, I will be glad to help: karenpryorpt@gmail.com.

Additional References
and Suggested Reading:

Ackerman, Sandra. (1992). *Discovering the Brain*. National Academy of Sciences. Washington DC. The National Academies Press.

Askenasy J. Lehmann J. (10 July 2013) Consciousness, Brain, Neuroplasticity retrieved from httpx://doi.org/103389/fspyg.2013.00412

Ayers, J., Robbins, J (2005). *Sensory Integration and the Child: 25th Anniversary Ed*. Western Psychological Services. Los Angeles, CA

Gould D., Fix J. *Board Review Series – Neuroanatomy*, (2008).Fourth Edition, Lippincott Williams & Wilkins, Maryland 2008, p. 177.

Blomberg, H., Dempsey, M. (2011). *Movements that heal: Rhythmic movement training and primitive reflex integration*. Sunnybank Hills, Qld.: Book Pal

Bickley, L., Szilagyi P., Bates B. (2013) *Bates' Guide to Physical Examination and History-Taking*. Philadelphia: Wolters Kluwer Health/Lippincott Williams & Wilkins.

Boyden ES, Katoh A, Raymond JL (2004). "Cerebellum-dependent learning: the role of multiple plasticity mechanisms". *Annu. Rev. Neurosci.* (**27**) 581–609.

Colledge N., Walker B., Ralston S (Eds.). (2010). *Davidson's principles and practice of medicine*. (21st ed.). Edinburgh: Churchill Livingstone/Elsevier. pp. 787, 1215–1217.

Carter R, Aldridge S, Page M, Parker S. (2009) *The Human Brain Book*. New York, NY: DK Publishing.

Corel JL. (1975) *The postnatal development of the human cerebral cortex*. Cambridge, MA; Harvard University Press.

Curtis, B.A., Jacobson, S. and Marcus, E.M. (1972) *An Introduction to the Neurosciences*, Philadelphia: W. B. Saunders.

Davis, M., Griessenauer, C., et al. The naming of the cranial nerves: A historical review. *Clinical Anatomy* **27** (1): 14–19.

Dehaene-Lambertz G, Montavont A, Jobert A, et al. (2009). Language or music, mother or Mozart? Structural and environmental influences on infants' language networks. *Brain and Language*. Retrieved from doi: 10.1016/j.bandl.2009.09.003.

DiPietro JA, Caulfield LE, Costigan KA, et al. (2004) Fetal Neurobehavioral development: a tale of two cities. *Developmental Psychology*. 40 (3): 445–56.

Dirix C, Nijhuis J, Jongsma H., et al. (2009) Aspects of fetal learning and memory. *Child Development*. 80(4):1251-1258.

Durston S, Casey BJ. (2006). What have we learned about cognitive development from neuroimaging? *Neuropsychologia*. 44:2149-2157.

Eccles J, Ito M, Szentágothai J (1967). *The Cerebellum as a Neuronal Machine*. Springer-Verlag P. 311.

Fitzgerald, M., FitzGerald T., et al. (2012). *Clinical neuroanatomy and neuroscience* (6th ed. ed.). [Edinburgh]: Saunders/Elsevier. p. 235.

Farroni T, Massaccesi S, Menon E, et al. (2007) Direct gaze modulates face recognition in young infants. *Cognition*.102:396-404.

Gilmore JH Lin W, Prasatwa M, et al. (2007) Regional gray matter growth, sexual dimorphism, and cerebral asymmetry in the neonatal brain. *Journal of Neuroscience.* 27(6):1255-1260.

Gopnic, Alison, Andrew N. Meltzoff, and Patricia K. Kuhl. (1999). *The Scientist in the Crib: What Early Learning Tells Us about the Mind.* New York, NY: HarperCollins.

Herschkowitz N. (2000) Neurological bases of behavioral development in infancy. *Brain & Development.* 22: 411–16.

Hobson, JA., Pace-Schott, E., Stickgold, R. (Dec 2000) Dreaming and the Brain: Toward a Cognitive Neuroscience of Conscious States. Retrieved from https://doi.org/10.1017/S0140525x00003976

Hobson JA. Pace-Schott EF. (2002) The Cognitive Neuroscience of Sleep: Neuronal Systems, Consciousness and Learning. Retrieved from https://www.nature.com/articles/nrn915

Hofer, Sabine; Frahm, Jens (2006). "Topography of the human corpus callosum revisited—Comprehensive fiber tractography using diffusion tensor magnetic resonance imaging". *NeuroImage* **32** (3): 989–94.

Holmboe K, Pasco Fearon RM, Csibra G, et al. (2008) Freeze-frame: a new infant inhibition task and its relation to frontal cortex tasks during infancy and early childhood. *Journal of Experimental Child Psychology.*100:89–114.

Hoon, A, Stashinko, E & Nagaw, L. et al. (2009) Sensory and motor deficits in children with cerebral palsy born preterm correlate with diffusion tensor imaging abnormalities in thalamocortical pathways. *Developmental Medicine and Child Neurology.* 51(9): 697-704

Kandel, E., Schwartz, J.,& Jessell T.(Eds.) (1991) *Principles of Neural Science*, 3rd Ed, New York: Appleton & Lange.

Kandel, E. R. (2013). *Principles of neural science* (5 th ed.). Appleton and Lange: McGraw Hill. pp. 1533–1549.

Knickmeyer RC, Gouttard S, Kang C, et al. (2008). A structural MRI study of human brain development from birth to 2 years. *Journal of Neuroscience*. 28 (47):12176–82.

Kurjak A, Pooh RK, Merce LT, et al. (2005).Structural and functional early human development assessed by three-dimensional and four-dimensional sonography. *Fertility and Sterility*. 84(5):1285-1299.

Lenroot R., Giedd J., Coch D (Ed), Fischer K (Ed), Dawson G (Ed)., (2007). The structural development of the human brain as measured longitudinally with magnetic resonance imaging. *Human behavior, learning, and the developing brain: Atypical development*. New York, NY: Guilford Press; 50-73.

Li Z, Sheng M. (2003) Some assembly required: the development of neuronal synapses. *Nature Reviews*. 4:833-841.

Lipina S., Colombo J., (2009) *Poverty and Brain Development During Childhood: An Approach From Cognitive Psychology and Neuroscience*. Washington, DC: American Psychological Association.

Mallatt, E.,. Marieb, P., Brady Wilhelm, J., (2012). *Human anatomy*. Boston: Benjamin Cummings. pp. 431–432.

Manuello J. Vercelli U, et al. (Feb 2016) Mindfulness Meditation and Consciousness: An Integrative Neuroscientific Perspective. Retrieved from https://doi.org/10.1016/j.concog.2015.12.005

Morgane PJ, Galler JR, Mokler DJ. (2005) A review of systems and networks of the limbic forebrain/limbic midbrain. *Progress in Neurobiology.* 75:143-160.

Mountcastle, V.B. (1968). *Medical Physiology, Vol. II,* 12th Ed, New York: Mosby..

Mtui, M.J. Turlough FitzGerald, Gregory Gruener, Estomih (2012). *Clinical neuroanatomy and neuroscience* (6th ed.). Saunders/Elsevier. p. 198, 220-222.

Nash, J., (Feb 3,1997) "Fertile Minds." *Time,* 48–51.

Nashner, LM, Shumway-Cook A, Matin O. (1983) Stance posture control in select groups of children with cerebral palsy: Deficits in sensory organization and muscular coordination. *Experimental Brain Research.* 49(3): 393-409.

Newberger, J., (1997). "New Brain Development Research–A Wonderful Window of Opportunity to Build Public Support for Early Childhood Education!" *Young Children* 52 (4): 4–7.

Norton, Neil (2007). *Netter's head and neck anatomy for dentistry.* Philadelphia, Pa.: Saunders Elsevier.

Nowakowski RS.(2006) Stable neuron numbers from cradle to grave. *Proceedings of the National Academy of Sciences of the United States of America.*103(33):12219-12220.

O'Connor, N., J. Talley, Simon (2009). *Clinical examination : a systematic guide to physical diagnosis* (6th ed.). Chatswood, N.S.W.: Elsevier Australia. pp. 330–352.

Player, M. Taylor J. et al, (2013). Neuroplasticity in Depressed Individuals Compared with Healthy Controls, *Neuropsychopharmacology,* 38, pp. 2101-2108

Reis, H., Collins W., Berscheid, E. (2000)"The Relationship Context of Human Behavior and Development." *Psychological Bulletin*, 126 (6): 844–72.

Rogers S.J., Vismara, L. et al, (2014). Autism Treatment in the First Year of Life: A Pilot Study of Infant Start, a Parent-Implemented Intervention for Symptomatic Infants *Journal of Autism and Developmental Disorders* 44, pp. 2981-2995

Russell D, Rosenbaum P, Cadman D, Gowland C, Hardy S, Jarvis S. (1989) The Gross Motor Function Measure: a means to evaluate the effects of physical therapy. *Developmental Medicine & Child Neurology* 31: 341–52.

Schmidt, R.F. (1986) *Fundamentals of Sensory Physiology*, 3rd Ed, New York: Springer-Verlag,.

Shamsiddini A. (2010) Comparison between the effect of neurodevelopmental treatment and sensory Integration therapy on gross motor function in children with cerebral palsy. *Iranian Journal of Child Neurology*. 4(1): 31-38

Shonkoff Jack, Deborah Phillips. (2000). *From Neurons to Neighborhoods: The Science of Early Childhood Development*. Institute of Medicine. The National Academies Press. Washington DC.

Shore, R. (1997). *Rethinking the Brain: New Insights into Early Development*. New York, NY: Families and Work Institute, pp. 26-27.

Standring, S., Borley, N.,. (2008). "Overview of cranial nerves and cranial nerve nuclei". *Gray's anatomy: the anatomical basis of clinical practice* (40th ed.). [Edinburgh]: Churchill Livingstone/ Elsevier.

Stefan, K. Kunesch E. et al. (2002) Mechanisms of Enhancement of Human Motor Cortex Excitability Induced b Interventional

Paired Associative Stimulation. *J Physiol.* Sept. 1; 543(Pt 2): 699-708.

Stefan, K., Wycislo, M., Classen J. (2004) Modulation of Associative Human Motor Cortical Plasticity by Attention. *J Neurophysiol.* July: 92(1):66-72. Retrieved from doi: 10.1152/jn.00383.2003

Striem-Amit E., Amedi, A. (2014). Visual Cortex Extrastriate Body-Selective Area Activation in Congenitally Blind People "Seeing" by Using Sounds, *Current Biology*, 24, pp. 687-692

Toda, T., Homma, D. et al (2013). Birth Regulates the Initiation of Sensory Map formation

Through Serotonin Signaling. *Developmental Cell*, Vol 27, Issue 1 p 32-46.

Vilensky, J., Robertson, W., Suarez-Quian, C. (2015). *The Clinical Anatomy of the Cranial Nerves: The Nerves of "On Olympus Towering Top".* Ames, Iowa: Wiley-Blackwell.

Webb S., Monk C., Nelson CA. (2001). Mechanisms of postnatal neurobiological development: implications for human development. *Developmental Neuropsychology.* 19(2):147-171.

Wiedenmayer C., Bansal R., Anderson G. et al. (2006) Cortisol Levels and Hippocampus Volumes in Healthy Preadolescent Children. *Biological Psychiatry.* 60:856-861.